ROUTLEDGE LIBRARY EDITIONS:
FREUD

Volume 2

CHRIST AND FREUD

CHRIST AND FREUD

A study of religious experience and observance

ARTHUR GUIRDHAM

Routledge
Taylor & Francis Group
LONDON AND NEW YORK

First published in 1959

This edition first published in 2014
by Routledge
27 Church Road, Hove BN3 2FA

Simultaneously published in the USA and Canada
by Routledge
711 Third Avenue, New York, NY 10017

Routledge is an imprint of the Taylor & Francis Group, an informa business

British Library Cataloguing in Publication Data
A catalogue record for this book is available from the British Library

ISBN: 978-0-415-83209-0 (Set)
eISBN: 978-1-315-85608-7 (Set)
ISBN: 978-0-415-71710-6 (Volume 2)
eISBN: 978-1-315-87151-6 (Volume 2)

Publisher's Note
The publisher has gone to great lengths to ensure the quality of this book but points out that some imperfections from the original may be apparent.

Disclaimer
The publisher has made every effort to trace copyright holders and would welcome correspondence from those they have been unable to trace.

Christ and Freud

A STUDY OF RELIGIOUS EXPERIENCE AND OBSERVANCE

ARTHUR GUIRDHAM

M. A., D. M., B. Sc. (Oxon), D. P. M.

Preface by Lawrence Durrell

Ruskin House

GEORGE ALLEN & UNWIN LTD

MUSEUM STREET LONDON

First published in 1959

Printed in Great Britain
in 11 on 12 Pilgrim type
by
East Midland Printing Company Limited,
Bury St. Edmunds, Peterborough, Kettering
and elsewhere

PREFACE

'On every front today the doctor as artist is on his way out,' wrote Dr Guirdham in his previous book, *A Theory of Disease*. I would prefer not to believe this somewhat gloomy statement, and indeed to plead that as long as there are doctors with his breadth of view and the liberal humanity of his outlook, so long shall medicine offer its best practitioners a chance to learn something of the enigmatic art (not science) upon which its foundations rest—the art of healing!

Dr Guirdham is a Vitalist by temperament and a psychiatrist by vocation, and his book issues, so to speak, not so much from his study as from the busy workshop of his daily practice; its implications concern the lay reader rather than the pure scientist and it can easily be followed by someone unversed in scientific terminology. This must be my excuse for appearing here in a prefatorial capacity—for I am no doctor, but simply a journeyman-writer actively interested in human values and what they mean. Dr Guirdham's thesis, despite its close reasoning and lucid presentation is not itself 'scientific' in the narrow deterministic sense, for he is only too well aware of the limitations of scientific method and subjects them to the scrutiny of a wise and enquiring mind. The questions he raises and probes deal, in fact, with the nature of health—psychic health—and its relationship to the whole complex of human ideas, but most narrowly to those of religion. They form his central topic. 'To estimate,' he writes, 'to what extent religious factors are important in relation to psychiatric conditions and more especially to neurosis.'

This book is, in a sense, both a pendant and an extension of the ideas set forth in *A Theory of Disease*, and his closely woven argument carries the reader across a far wider field than that of psychiatry—as the title of his first chapter ('Christ and Freud') will show. It is the work of a natural philosopher who is also a doctor, and thus it has a double claim upon our attention, for it is no tissue of opinionations but the expression of a philosophy of medicine.

While he does not spare atrophied theologies, whether scientific or religious, he is anxious to isolate and preserve those creative elements which so often lie buried in the accumulations of detritus thrown up around such giant mental constructs. For both science and religion tend to lose impetus and harden into dogma, to atrophy. Dr Guirdham belongs to that small band of creative individuals who feel bound to sort through these huge slag heaps in search of whatever gold may lie underneath the dross. And his long clinical practice has enabled him to test his views in the field, so to speak—the field of the human personality, which is so deeply influenced by the very views it holds (or is taught) about its own nature. Some of these views come from science, some from religion. How valid are they and how acceptable today? To what extent do they prejudice or nourish the health of the individual human psyche? Could our illnesses be regarded as metaphysical extensions of our beliefs? Where does the doctor's practice touch and merge with that of the priest?

These important questions and many others are canvassed here with sympathy, wit and insight. No artist concerned with values could fail to be fascinated by this book; nor could any religious person who was concerned with the theological foundations of belief. And to those doctors who might feel trapped in the labyrinth of obsolete scientific dogma Dr Guirdham's penetrating modesty should bring new hope, a new attitude to the problems of health and disease.

Perhaps, after all, the doctor as artist is just beginning to emerge.

LAWRENCE DURRELL

CONTENTS

PART THREE: GUILT AND CLERICALISM

PART FOUR
FREEDOM AND CAPTIVITY

INTRODUCTION

The aim of this book is to study the psychiatric foundations of religion and also, conversely, to estimate to what extent religious factors are important in relation to psychiatric conditions and more especially to neurosis. Most readers will know that Freud regarded religion as a manifestation of neurosis and as a sign of man's emotional adolescence. The author rejects this view. He regards the Freudian theories as valid explanations of much organized religion but as completely inadequate to account for religious experience. Whatever Freudian doctrine may say of man's emotional immaturity it is, itself, in its attitude to religion, a manifestation of spiritual retardation.

My object in writing this introductory note is to issue a warning. The defenders of religion often argue that it is an innate need. This contention plays into the hands of the opposition. All religions and philosophical systems should be scrutinized carefully to see to what degree they satisfy human needs. The more rapidly and neatly they do so the more one should be suspicious of their ultimate truth, though not of their immediate usefulness. Even though they may be fallacious, if they bring peace to a minority they are serving an immense purpose. One can even say that they are true for the particular kind of individual to whom they are especially accommodated, in the same way as certain forms of medical treatment are especially valid in certain illnesses in certain people. One is, however, doing no good service to religion in labouring that it fulfils a need. In the last analysis what we are concerned with is whether religious experience is real or illusory.

Now we cannot produce evidence for the reality of religious experience by any intellectual balance sheet of pros and cons such as the scientist uses in establishing the truth of a particular theory. Where religion is based on intellectual, theological or historical proof its nature has been misunderstood and its form perverted. Attempts to teach religion by adducing so-called scientific proof of its validity are especially deadly and their effect on the spiritual life of the individual is stultifying. The highest wisdom of the world has never been presented in a form palatable to the exponents of the scientific method as we understand it. The doctrines of Christ, Buddha and the Hindu sages are offered to the world not as neat and intellectually irrefutable propositions of Euclid but as systems to be tested by us so that we learn from actual experience whether they are true or no. (The same applies to psycho-analytical doctrine. You can prove by scientific methods that hydrogen and oxygen combined produce water but you cannot by the same methods prove that the repression of an instinct produces emotional conflict. You can only apply the doctrine as widely as possible and see if it fits the facts.)

Religion is emphatically not to be established by any form of theorising. That is the whole point. It is either a truth of experience or nothing. But it is a truth which can only be attained by a process of self-annihilation. It is only when man has shed his egotistical self and with it his needs that he is open to a truth not specially moulded by himself nor determined by his needs. If the truth which comes to us when we are detached from ourselves is the same as is perceived by others vastly different from us in race and creed and separated from us in time then we are as near as we can ever be to absolute truth, even considered by the most rigid standards of science. In the course of this book I deal with the phenomena constant in mystical experience. Here I need only emphasise that what rests on observation and experience is, in terms of commonsense, of more sure foundation than the convenient and extremely useful abstractions of scientific method.

In this book I talk of self-annihilation and, at the same time, of how a higher self, of which the individual is acutely aware, is realized in the course of religious experience. There is nothing contradictory in this though at first sight it may appear slightly confusing. The self to be annihilated is that formed from the social and dynamic personalities. It is only when this is achieved that the higher Self can be realized.

PART ONE

Christ and Freud

I

THE RELIGIOUS ASPECT OF PSYCHIATRIC ILLNESS

Man's attitude to God, the Absolute, or whatever he choses to call the universal conception he either worships or shrinks from, is probably the most important of his co-ordinated reactions. The fact that he may have consciously excluded religion from his life does not invalidate this contention. The more ferociously he pursues the path of materialism the more evident his reaction against more universal and timeless conceptions. The atheist would not so bitterly inveigh against God if, with some part of his being, he did not believe in His existence. One does not fulminate against nothing. Nor would the agnostic argue so convincingly and at such length the necessity of doubt if he were not himself struggling against some inward conviction. Very often men reason best in defence of the indefensible.

Many may be inclined to question the part religion, or our negation of it, plays in our lives. Until recent times it was taboo in our Anglo-Saxon civilization to discuss the three subjects of God, death and money. The fact that such a strong embargo was exercised in our Protestant mercantile society emphasises the degree to which the three subjects were still of immense importance to us.

When I say that our acceptance or negation of religion is a fundamental factor in our lives I am not referring to the teachings of any particular creed or sect but to the maintenance or abandonment of a religious attitude towards life. By this latter phrase I imply that the individual does not regard himself as a self-contained entity with complex social relationships, but as a part of the universal spirit which is in all things and which exists beyond considerations of space and time.

If we believe in the importance of our attitude towards religion we are bound to accept that the relationship between the latter and psychiatry is of vital significance. Psychiatry is concerned with the disorders of our intellectual and emotional life. It stands, therefore, in the closest relation to our religious attitude, seeing that the latter is the strongest factor tending to co-ordinate and harmonize these psychological processes. Now the importance of the religious factor obtrudes itself at every turn in our observation of the psychologically sick and especially of the neurotic. For the benefit of those without psychiatric knowledge, if such persons still exist against a cultural background which confers on the individuals belonging to it a little knowledge and less understanding of a lot of subjects, it may be profitable to define the different varieties of neurosis. There are first the anxiety states characterised by increased tension, by indefinable feelings of dread, by special phobias of heights, closed spaces and disease, and by those physical disturbances, consequent on anxiety, which are known as somatic symptoms. Secondly, we have the obsessional states which specially affect the over-conscientious and which are often accompanied by ritualistic actions and compulsive thoughts which appear to be forced on the individual against his own will. Thirdly, there are the hysterical conditions in persons of heightened suggestibility. These latter, at the present time, express themselves most commonly in the form of what appear to be physical symptoms but which have no organic foundation. There are also the states of neurotic depression which are either reactive to adverse circumustances or long-standing anxiety, or which have their basis in the glandular and biochemical constitution of the individual. Compared with the psychoses, or mental diseases, the neuroses do not cause any dramatic deterioration in the personality of the individual, who is able to maintain his place in society. In this book I am chiefly concerned, so far as my study of psychiatric illness is concerned, with the neuroses.

Probably all neurotic conditions, together with a large proportion of the psychoses, exhibit a common factor which stands in the closest relation to one of the most fundamental attributes of religious experience. This common finding is the victim's excessive and painful consciousness of his own personality.[1] In phases of health and happiness our consciousness of our personalities is relatively minimal. All neurotic states are manifestations of insecurity, and what is a sense of insecurity but a perception of ourselves as unpleasantly separated from God, from our fellows and nakedly apart from the world we live in? The patient suffering from phobias is painfully reminded of his own vulnerable and separate existence when he quails from crossing an open space, an action performed without thought and effort by individuals not so afflicted. Most states of severe depression, whether neurotic or psychotic in nature, are accompanied by intense self-accusation, in which the individual blames himself, with a ferocious absence of logic, for sins he has never committed or faults he has never exhibited. Self-accusation is the dire apotheosis of self-consciousness. All symptoms of all diseases, whether psychiatric or physical, are manifestations of a heightened perception of ourselves as individuals. Physical pain, for example, is a sharp reminder of our separate existence.

The neuroses are specific forms of unhappiness manifested in the form of disease symptoms and, in their purest development, in the absence of immediately tangible causes. But what we have said about the individual's painfully heightened perception of himself applies to all forms of unhappiness not honoured by the spurious dignity of medical nomenclature. We may indeed go further and say, to take the converse case, that man's greatest happiness is experienced in those moments when his perception of himself as a separate individuality is at its lowest. In love, in its spiritual aspect, the individual annihilates himself in contemplation of the adored object. In physical love,

[1] When I speak of self-awareness I am referring to the subject's perception of the personality of his desires, ambitions and sentiments, in fact to the self, in the mundane sense of the word, as understood by the average individual with no introspective endowments and no special religious or philosophical inclinations. I am emphatically not referring to the ecstatic self-awareness which accompanies certain states of mysticism or enlightenment and which is indeed the total opposite of the condition we are considering.

where it reaches the plane of ecstacy, the individuals concerned achieve the benediction of self-forgetfulness in a crescendo of shared sensation. The effect of great art, or of beauty in any form adored by the observer, is to induce a state of being lost, often described by the individual as 'being taken out of himself.' All happiness is a little death, in which the individual abandons for the moments of its duration the conglomeration of desires, sentiments and ambitions which go to make up his personality. Even the successful accomplishment of desire itself ensures its own death. Love, which in one form or another is regarded as the greatest blessing with which the individual can be endowed, involves the annihilation of his awareness of his separate existence.

Now while, in psychiatry, we are confronted with increased awareness of personality, it is only in religion that we find emphasised the importance of the opposite condition of non-selfconsciousness. All the great religions of the world, and for my purposes I refer especially to Christianity, Buddhism and the Hindu faiths, insist on the necessity of the individual seeking self-obliteration by absorption in God or the Absolute. By self-obliteration I do not mean the performance of unselfish acts or stressful, purposive and often unsuccessful attempts to think of others rather than oneself. So-called good works are often among the most self-conscious acts performed by the individual. As he goes slumming or on his errands of mercy the individual may be all too conscious of himself engaged in an occupation which may be an effort and against the grain. By self-obliteration I am trying to convey that perception of oneself as a dimly apprehended instrument of a more universal influence rather than as a separately functioning personality. In the three religions mentioned above self-surrender is not only implied in their basic creeds but, in addition, specific techniques are encouraged to facilitate the development of such a state of enlightenment. In Christianity we may study the methods advocated by St Ignatius Loyola, or practice meditation or go into retreats. Unfortunately these methods are less developed in Christianity than in the other two great religions. In Buddhism contemplative exercises are recommended in which the individual is enabled to shed his conception of himself as a separate individuality. The aim of some of these exercises is to change the subject's attitude to his own body so that he sees it not as a personal possession but as a fortuitious collection of organs and tissues. In certain of the Hindu faiths the practice of Yoga encourages the devoté to lose his individuality in merging with the universal spirit.

There is therefore a strong case for the utilization of the methods of religion in the treatment of psychiatric disorders. Perhaps, so far as the neuroses are concerned, the individual cannot be considered on safe ground until he has recaptured or redeveloped a religious attitude. It is therefore important that we should examine the present relations existing between psychiatric and religious opinion.

When I speak of psychiatry I am referring to the psychotherapeutic techniques based on the analytical doctrines of Freud, Adler, Jung and others. This approach is especially concerned with the relationship between underlying emotional states and manifested disease symptoms. The so-called dynamic methods, which include insulin shock and electric convulsive therapy, are not relevant to this thesis. Where psychotherapeutic techniques are employed they are based essentially on the findings of the analytical school. This is true whether the psychiatrist employs the classical method of psychoanalysis, or whether he limits himself to psychotherapy on a more superficial level or to abreactive treatment with the aid of drugs. Whatever the form of psychotherapy favoured, the psychiatrist is employing the principles of psychoanalytic theory as laid down by Freud, Adler and Jung, and more especially, by the first-named. Our discussion reduces itself to a study of the present relations existing between psychoanalytic and religious opinion.

II

SOME PSYCHIATRIC MECHANISMS IN RELIGIOUS OBSERVANCE

When I refer to religion it should be understood that for the purposes of this argument I am dealing mainly with Christianity. This is for several reasons. Psychoanalysis arose against the background of an at any rate officially Christian Europe. Its principles have been applied for the most part in Europe and in the overseas countries founded by settlers from this continent. Secondly, in comparison with what obtains in Christian countries, the neuroses are of far less incidence in Buddhist and Hindu communities. The practice of psychoanalysis is less in the latter communities because they have less need for it. In considering psychoanalytical principles mainly in relation to Christianity it may be objected that Freud himself was a Jew. Be this as it may, he lived and practised against a background of orthodox Christianity. Furthermore, as we shall show later, orthodox Christianity has never been thoroughly emancipated from the shackles of Judaism from which Christ sought to free it.

Let us deal first with the attitude of the exponents of psycholanalysis towards religion. Though this has been modified in recent years, it is incontrovertible that originally psychoanalytic teaching insisted that religion was essentially a myth produced by man for his own comfort. Freud, in writing on this subject, was sufficiently convinced to entitle his thesis 'The Future of an Illusion'. His argument was, briefly, that religion was a kind of mass obsessional neurosis. He compared the ritual of religion, with its constant repetition of certain actions and phrases, with the compulsive actions and thoughts of the obsessional neurotic. According to Freud, to touch one railing in three as one passes down the street, or to be careful to walk on all the lines between the stones of the pavement, are actions essentially similar in origin to passing one's fingers through holy water. Similarly, to be afflicted by the recurring fear that one might commit suicide shares a common psychological causation with the repetition of certain phrases in the Litany. Religion and the obsessional neurosis are held to have a common basis in a sense of guilt. The latter is usually said to have its origin in shame derived from infantile sexual experiences. Both religion and obsessional neurosis require an atoning ritual. In the case of the former this is provided for in the liturgy and by acts of atonement and the performance of penances. In the obsessional state the placating of the Evil Eye is achieved through the characteristic compulsive thoughts and actions. Heaven, to Freud, is a form of wish fulfilment. We believe in its existence because without such a belief life on this earth would be altogether too bleak. Similarly God, the Father, is an infinite projection of our own male parent, infinitely wise and benevolent if he is loved, or all-powerful if he is accepted with reservations. The emotional energy available for the purposes of religion is derived from the suppression, or partial suppression, of the sexual instinct by the process of sublimation.

It should be made clear that in the ensuing paragraphs I am discussing religion in the doctrinal as distinct from the mystical sense of the term. I am concerned with the observances and the theological structure of organized religion as we know it. This is for the simple reason that Freud himself only considered religion in this light. To him revealed religion and the direct experience of God did not exist, except as illusory phenomena. It will be seen later that this was the cardinal error of the Freudian system. Naturally the phenomena of mystical and revealed religion occur within the limits of organized creeds. It is, indeed, the aim of the more enlightened leaders of orthodox opinion to open the hearts of their followers to direct experience of God. But in this section one can only refer to religion in the terms mentioned above, because these are the limits of controversy imposed by Freud himself.

It is quite impossible to devote time to the examination of the Freudian view of religion from the point of view of psychiatric theory. The possibilities of the subject are endless. I think, however, it would be useful to mention an inconsiderable fraction of the historical and clinical evidence relevant to the subject.

The history of religion is as old as man. Even at his most primitive he has felt the need for systems of religious belief. We should allow that these systems may be as much a part of man's adaptation to a hostile environment as are the changes in the physical and mental habits he has manifested in the course of his history. At his most primitive, and where the threats to his integrity have been thunder and lightning and the cruder forces of nature, the religious observances of men have been embryonic and unsystematized. They have consisted of simple propitiatory offerings and gestures. The first of these latter, like the offerings of food and slaughtered animals, were as physical and crude as the pattern of his life. Where the dangers to which he has been exposed have become less crude and physical, the religious observances of man have become more theological and systematized and have manifested themselves in prayers and penances. The mere fact that religion is of antique origin and has been constantly present in man's history is no proof of its validity. From many aspects it can be conceived of as anodyne and a protection, the form of which has varied according to the different ways in which man has viewed his always vulnerable condition.

Religion as conceived of by Freud is a neurosis and the latter condition is invariably associated with a sense of insecurity. Now one of the classical methods used by the individual to escape from this predicament is to submit himself to the discipline and protection of systems of ideas. For the most part religious systems are better than their secular counterparts in serving this purpose. At the present time political systems only serve this purpose in so far as they are primarily religious and secondarily political. The Nazi movement had all the attributes of a religious creed and was endowed with a fervour and fanaticism which had not been seen in Europe since the wars of religion and which exceeded these latter in barbarism. To regard the Nazi movement as a kind of specialized political disturbance manipulated by thugs is to fail to comprehend one of the most significant lessons of the last few centuries. It spread with epidemic virulence in a nation more prone to neurosis than any other in Europe and which has for long produced a more than normal quota of adolescent suicides and other manifestations of maladjustment. Communism, too, has all the attributes of an organized religion. It has a rigid system of ideas, many of them rudimentary and of limited scope, but for which an universal application is demanded. It does not permit its followers ideas about its ideas and in different moral situations its ethical standards are dizzily varying. It is of great significance that in a largely agnostic age the attraction of religious systems is so strong that the only political movements with any ardour have converted themselves into religious creeds.

In the course of history it is all too obvious how the exponents of organized religion have used their particular creeds as a buttress for their own insecurity. The ferocity with which they have defended themselves against the adverse criticism of even minor deviationists is illuminating. The naturally irreligious can be distinguished by the fury with which they support the articles of religion. Stable individuals do not display towards those who differ from them signs of intolerance, let alone those of vindictiveness. Still less do those, genuinely secure in the love of God, exhibit the signs of fear and insecurity which are the basis of religious persecution. In the last analysis it is questionable if the truly religious have beliefs at all, in the intellectual sense of the term. One of the final stages of dedication is when the individual surrenders even his beliefs in the cause of trust and resignation. Faith is a reaction of the whole being and not an act of intellectual subservience.

Men have wondered for centuries how Christians can have tortured and killed each other, for the love of God, and what intricate variety of spiritual blindness could have enabled the Inquisition to burn devout Christians in the name of Christ. Modern psychiatry permits us to see that the Inquisitors were themselves, below the conscious level, afflicted with doubt. Men so doubting, and reacting with guilt towards their uncertainty, could atone and reassure themselves either by the punishment of themselves or others. In such circumstances the choice of self-castigation or the chastisement of others depends on the temperament of the individual. The flagellants were recruited from the former and the Inquisitors from the latter class.

Though I have, in the last paragraph, mentioned specifically the aberrations of Christians, there is nothing in it which does not apply equally to the persecutions which have stained the reputations of other religious systems. It is to be feared that the religions originating in the Middle East have a worse record than the others. This is due to a particular veneration for systems of ideas which seems to afflict the Semitic races and which reflects itself equally in Christians, Jews and the followers of Mahomet. The Far Eastern religions, where truth is something acquired as a result of certain slowly acquired states of being, have till now indulged far less in persecution.

Whenever a sect proclaims that its own creed is the sole prescription for salvation it should be assumed that its basis is neurotic and rests on fear and a sense of insecurity. The more the individual is obsessed by his own insecurity the more he is likely to chose a rigid and infallible prescription for salvation. This exclusiveness is the bane of Christianity when considered in relation to the Hindu and Buddhist faiths. Christianity insists on the doctrine of salvation through Christ alone. Few Roman Catholics would qualify this view and quite recently the head of the Anglican community expressed himself positively to this effect. It is the boast of Christianity that no other religion is so supported by the evidence of history. This insistence is useful as a proof of its validity but from the spiritual aspect is quite undesirable. A sense of the presence of God as everywhere and within the individual can be achieved by many different approaches, including some not exclusively religious. When one considers the extraordinary number of Christian sects, many claiming exclusive ownership of the keys of the Kingdom, one sees to what degree Christianity is saturated with the belief in its own specific remedies. It also cannot be doubted that the incidence of neurosis in the Christian world is higher than in the less exclusive Buddhist and Hindu communities.

Perhaps the most important psychiatric factor in organized Christianity is a sense of guilt. It has been well said that Christianity is an attempt to escape from guilt and Buddhism a means of escaping sorrow. I have left the discussion of the element of guilt in Christianity to the section which deals with the particular tendency of the latter religion to induce neurotic reactions. What I have written in the previous paragraphs applies not only to Christianity but to any religious system where intellectually derived theological considerations are predominant. It is enough to say here that a sense of guilt to a neurotic degree has been obvious in the history of the more extreme Protestant sects since their foundation. Calvin found even a smile to be intolerable on Sundays. In our own country dancing and games were, under the Commonwealth, classified not only as sins but in some cases as illegal. To the extreme wing of the Plymouth Brethren dancing and the theatre are still sinful. It is not that pleasure is avoided as being a distraction in a life of religious contemplation. This could hardly be so as most of the Brethren are Marthas rather than Marys. The underlying principle is that a regime of mental self-mutilation is as necessary for salvation as the cessation of smoking and eating pastries is in preparing for the Boat Race. Combined with this ethic of castration is a belief in a literal and picturesque hell where the evil doer will be punished for attendance at dance halls. The underlying neurosis which produces such a colourful theology requires no further emphasis.

To anyone with even a non-professional interest in human nature certain neurotic features, directly related to the religious observances they undertake, are to be observed in a considerable proportion of churchgoers. It cannot be denied that Freud's views on the origins of religion apply with sinister accuracy to many who call themselves religious. In many earnest and flamboyant practitioners of religion the underlying sense of guilt reveals itself, as a form of projection, in a ferocious and inquisitional interest in the sins of others. The devout magistrate, often of evangelical or nonconformist loyalties, who doles out sentences, with chill ferocity, for minor infringements of the moral code, is a familiar type. Naturally people influenced in their conduct by such psychiatric mechanisms are scattered widely through the community as a whole but it cannot be denied that the religious moralist, dressed in a little brief authority and titillated by the joys of inflicting punishment, is a classical type and part of the stock in trade of our religious and legal system. At the opposite end of the scale we encounter many practitioners of the more ritualistic forms of religion, such as Anglo- and Roman Catholicism, whose main concern is to dissipate their desire to atone in a complicated and, if possible, colourful ceremonial. Once this has been done, in the form of regular religious observance, the particular species under discussion lead lives so hedonistic and so blissfully immune from simple ethical considerations that one wonders if their masses and penances are a prophylactic enabling them to live in between times in a condition of comfortable egoism.

It has been said that religion is a veiled and myth engendered symbol of security designed to prevent man from contemplating with pain his own defencelessness. Support is provided for this view by observation of those individuals in whom strict orthodoxy, especially in relation to the belief in personal survival, is combined with a preoccupation with worldly security and especially with money. There are so many people whose fanatical preoccupation with their place in the world to come seems a logical extension of the prosperity they have been so careful to preserve in this. Religion should always be regarded as suspect if it reinforces too directly and mathematically some obvious flaw in the patient's psychological armoury. It should be remembered that many neurotic patients actually gain by their symptoms, however much these latter may at first sight seem painful and crippling. Their neuroses enable them to endure the relative comforts of self-deception and fantasy in place of the bleaker reality of seeing themselves and the world in their true outlines. Similarly, religious practices which too adroitly provide a poultice for the patient's more immediate wounds are to be regarded as equally self-deceiving as neurotic symptoms and as partaking of the same nature.

It is in the matter of belief in Heaven and in personal survival that we find in so many believers the signs of neurotic evasion. Practitioners of religion, for whom a belief in Heaven and immortality, and, for that matter, in God Himself, are necessary because without such beliefs life would be a meaningless and unjust chaos, should be scrutinized carefully for the signs of neurosis and self-deception. It is much to be doubted whether any person seeking rewards from religion can be regarded as truly religious. Certainly his spiritual potentialities must have definite limits. We should be concerned with religion for God's sake and not for our own. This is the very heart of the matter, to count ourselves as nothing, and when I say to count ourselves as nothing I mean this in its literal and not in any relative sense. In the service of God, or in submission to the Absolute, we are unable to expect anything for ourselves except to be merged in the only unity. The more we are absorbed the more we are extinguished. The person whose religion rests chiefly on belief in personal survival and the reward of heaven is merely utilising well-worn and well-established psychological mechanisms for comfort and self-delusion.

But, it will be asked, who bases his religion on such considerations? In my experience those who ask this question with the greatest indignation are those who are most guilty in this matter. No one can answer such a question with certainty but I would say in all sincerity that I believe that for the majority of practising Christians their religion is founded on a belief in personal survival and in some kind of heaven, not necessarily conceived of as something spatial. This is not to say that these beliefs are either peculiar to Christianity or its fundamental essence. I am merely stating that the two factors named are of prime importance in influencing the beliefs of the majority of orthodox Christians, no matter to what sect they belong. After all, evidence is constantly provided by the all-too revealing statements made by the leaders of the Churches. In a Sunday newspaper there has recently been a series of articles by eminent individuals on survival after death. It is perhaps natural but I think, too, a little deplorable that a succession of essays purporting to be religious should be devoted to such a subject. Of all questions related to religion that of personal survival is one of the least fundamental. It is significant that among all the writers only the Buddhist made this point. This is not to say that the writer does not believe in some form of personal survival. He merely asserts that this state, if achieved, would be a by-product of the religious life and not one of its cardinal aims. It is very significant that the argument that personal immortality and the reward of Heaven were obligatory beliefs, because without them life would be meaningless, was laboured to a greater degree by a very eminent ecclesiastic than by any of his fellow contributors among the laity.

Too many among us have heard sermons in which the question as to whether Christ was resurrected and appeared after death to His disciples is regarded as the central point of Christianity.[2] In recent years, in a village church of the Anglican persuasion, the preacher stated that Christ was either the Son of God or the greatest imposter the world has even seen. Many readers must have heard similar fulminations on the

[2] Had Christ regarded His resurrection as the central point of His doctrine, He would have best ensured its acceptance by returning after His crucifixion to live among men. Why did He appear only to a chosen few? Surely this was to demonstrate, to those capable of understanding, not the truth of personal survival but the triumph of spirit over matter. When He ascended into Heaven surely it was not to prove anything about personal immortality in the positive sense but to demonstrate its relative unimportance compared with the fundamentals of His doctrine. It is probably human fallability and weakness which has over-emphasized the importance of a personal resurrection and has to a large extent failed to grasp its true significance. Christ rejected the huge, dramatic chance of a new ministry on earth to illustrate the importance of a spirituality beyond all considerations of immortality as we commonly understand it.

same theme. It is hardly to be credited that such emotional and histrionic views have their origin in genuine religious feeling. It is a good rule that theological opinions expressed with force should be regarded as suspect. The inner harmony, induced by genuine religious feeling, does not lend itself to the diatribe. Such pronouncements, deriving ultimately from the fear of personal extinction, are analogous to the bellicose self-confidence which is a compensation for inferiority feelings.

The relationship between a belief in personal immortality and a dread of extinction was vividly brought home to me by an old, very experienced and very skilled doctor of my acquaintance. He said that of the many deaths he had seen practically all were peaceful and without any element of terror. Among the unfortunate minority was a high proportion of clerics. It is horrifying to think that those who, of all men, should be merged in God should, at the end, be struggling violently to retain their own personality. Can it be that these men's very choice of vocation was a form of insurance against the horrors of personal extinction?

So far as the social aspects of religion are concerned, it is not difficult to observe in many of those addicted to good works either a desire to dominate others, expressed either directly in a will to power or, more obliquely, in an obsessive preoccupation with the pleasures of martyrdom.

The psychiatric mechanisms observed in these few religious types I have described are commonplace. I have mentioned them merely to emphasize their frequent incidence in those devoted to religious observances. It might be argued that this is a matter of no importance and that neurotic phenomena are so common in all spheres of existence that their occurrence among the religious is of no significance. But, as may be more obvious later, religious experience should be our best safeguard against the inroads of neurosis. The facts mentioned above indicate that the protective power of ordinary church-going Christianity is not adequate because the religious experience accompanying it is not sufficiently deep.

III

CRITICISM OF THE PSYCHO-ANALYTICAL INTERPRETATION OF RELIGION

I have now produced a certain amount of evidence to show that, according to the principles of psychoanalysis, religion is a mass reaction based on neurotic mechanisms. I will now consider the errors committed by psychoanalytic theory in its attempts to mine the foundations of religion.

In the first place we must point out that religion must of necessity employ for its expression the mental and emotional attributes we possess. It needs a machinery for its manifestation just as bodies are needed for propagation. The fact that certain well-established psychiatric mechanisms are utilized in religious feeling does not in any sense imply that the latter is neither genuine nor divine. Many medical students, hitherto believers, pass through crises of doubt when they realise that certain glands and biochemical reactions influence strongly the moods and emotions of the individual. They learn, too, how certain diseases like general paralysis and disseminate sclerosis can affectradically the character of the patient.[3]

To abandon one's faith on these grounds is equivalent to so doing because of the existence in the world of disease, death and sorrow. These latter calamities were as much or more existent in Europe in the ages of faith as they are in this epoch of scientific inquiry. It is no unique discovery that these universal calamities have each their separate mechanisms. All science has done has been to elucidate the nature of the latter. It cannot claim to have discovered the self-evident fact of the existence of tragedy. If we accept that some men are rendered illogically hopeful by pulmonary tuberculosis and others depressed by jaundice, I do not see why we should be unduly perturbed that religion, which involves our mental and emotional life, should depend for its expression on the mechanisms elucidated by modern psychiatry. The nature of

[3] There is a certain amount of evidence that a contrary mechanism is at work in certain organic diseases of the nervous system and that the pre-existing nature of the individual can influence the type of disease manifested. Given a syphilitic infection of the nervous system the physically compact extroverted types are more prone to general paralysis than their more elongated introverted brethren, who, for the most part, opt for locomotor ataxia.

man is such that, when confronted with a new hypothesis as to his nature, he for the most part limits himself to three reactions. The majority disregard it completely. Others, secure in their established religious and ethical systems, reject it entirely as a threat to their comfort and security. Others, in a revolt against authority which derives from their earlier revolt against a repressive parent, see in it a personal contribution to their own emancipation. Only a tiny majority sees the new thesis as a contribution to human experience, as one may observe a new leaf opening on an old tree.

It may be argued that I am here begging the question and that the psychiatric mechanisms involved in organized religion are essentially abnormal. But there is no clear lines of demarcation between the neurotic and the illusory category we call the normal. Both exhibit throughout their lives the same psychiatric mechanisms. The neurotic is distinguished not by any completely unique system of reactions but by a preference for some particular mechanisms at the expense of others and by his incapacity to free himself of the mechanisms of his choice.

IV

SEXUAL SYMBOLISM IN RELIGION

There is no need to withdraw what has been said as to the obsessional element in religion and of the feelings of guilt and insecurity which provide the impetus for so many religious reactions. It is when we come to the question of sublimation that we find that the psychoanalytic approach must be employed with caution. Whereas earlier in this chapter I have dealt with religion in its organized, orthodox and doctrinal aspect, in the ensuing paragraphs it will be necessary to consider also the question of mystical and directly revealed religion. That religious feeling may depend to a large extent on the repression and deviation of the sex instinct does not imply that it is neither genuine nor normal. The religious impulse is not regarded by psychiatrists as deriving from an inborn primary instinct. It is therefore not surprising that it must demand for its expression the utilization of one or other of the more powerful and basic instincts. It is therefore only to be expected that the sex instinct is called into play in the genesis of religious feeling. It would indeed be more surprising if the truth were otherwise, because it is not altogether easy to see what part such an instinct as that of self-assertion could play in the production of religious feeling.

It is often argued that the sexual allusions, in the writings of the saints and mystics, is so blatantly obvious that religious activity of this nature must be a fairly direct substitute for sexuality. This view is quite erroneous. The very fact that the allusions are so obvious renders this view invalid. Most manifestations of repression express themselves in a much more veiled form. The fact is that the nomenclature of earthly love is the nearest available mechanism for the expression of its divine equivalent. It has been used throughout the centuries by mystics to describe their communion with God and Christ. There is no need to quote from the voluminous evidence provided by the recorded visions of the saints and mystics, or from mystical poetry such as that of Thomas Traherne. There is, however, an interesting example of the expression of religious mysticism in a more concealed and allegorical form. This example is all the more interesting because it reveals how such an allegorical approach can for centuries deceive men as to its real implications. I am referring to the true significance of the songs of the troubadours. To anyone with a superficial knowledge of these poets their productions were love songs dedicated to the mistresses for whom they pined. But the theme of those songs is overwhelmingly that of unrequited, that is to say unfilled, love. In the great majority of cases these poems were addressed to women of higher social status than the authors and hence, from the symbolic point of view, to be regarded as unattainable. Recent research has shown that the castles in which these women lived were strongholds of the Albigensian faith. Now among the fundamentals of the latter faith were the beliefs that the flesh was innately sinful, that even the physical celebration of marriage was deleterious and that the procreation of children into a world of sin was deplorable. There is considerable evidence that the castles in which the objects of the troubadour's verses lived were in many cases centres of the Albigensian faith. It is now considered possible that these poems were addressed to a single female Holy Spirit with which their authors desired to be merged. It is of striking significance that the motives of the fathers of European poetry should have been misconstrued so radically throughout eight or nine centuries.

Perhaps the most important fact to be derived from study of the utilization of sexual imagery in religion is that on the whole this is far less direct and infinitely more veiled in ordinary religion based on ritual and dogma than in the ecstatic experiences of the saints and mystics. Those who instinctively distrust mystical experience will see in this exactly what they expected. Indeed it cannot be denied that some so-called mystics have presented the signs of hysteria, the signs and symptoms of which have been markedly coloured with sexuality. The true mystic, without hysterical tendencies, may still express himself in terms saturated with sexuality. On the other hand the orthodox believer and the ecclesiastics presiding over him practise for the most part a form of religious observance in which sexual imagery is not crudely manifest. Where it occurs it is more or less masked and in most cases the believer is unaware of its existence or implications. The sexual element is, in fact, repressed and to some extent at least the religious observance associated with it is sexually derived and a result of sublimation.

We must consider a further fact of the first importance. For the greater part of Christian history orthodox believers in general have distrusted the mystic indulging in his or her florid use of sexual imagery. In addition, the general attitude of the hierarchy towards mystics has been at the least coercive and paranoid and at worst persecutory to the degree of savagery. Many Christian mystics, as, for instance, Meister Eckhard (1270-1327) were interrogated by the Inquisition. Even great saints recognised in their lifetime as such, like St Teresa of Avila, were subjected to severe interrogation and advised to disregard their experiences of reality. The excuse of the apologists for the inquisitors is, of course, that they were endeavouring with all charity and fraternal love to protect the souls of the saints from the contamination of heresy. But such precautions are superfluous in dealing with mystics, seeing that these latter derive their religion not from dogma or any variety of intellectual concept, but from actual experience of the presence of God. The psychological mechanisms involved in the attitude of the orthodox religionist to the saint and mystic is very familiar. We have that always suspect interest in sexuality in others, in the name of morality or virtue, which so often indicates repressed sexuality in those who constitute themselves ethical tribunals on the subject of sex. At the same time it should be remembered that the frank and uninhibited use of sexual imagery by the saints and mystics may well be evidence that they did not suffer from the same repressed sexuality as their persecutors.

In a book of this size it is utterly impossible to give even the barest outlines of the relationship between the sexual impulse and religious feeling. One can only state, as a bold summary of the particular question we are discussing, that while the evidence is that sublimation of the sex instinct plays a great part in religious experience, this mechanism is not necessarily abnormal. Furthermore, while the rôle of repressed sexuality in orthodox, theologically-directed religion is undoubted, in revealed religion the part it plays is probably minimal, in spite, or because, of the florid imagery employed by the mystic.

I do not propose to deal at this juncture with what to me is the most telling evidence against Freud's interpretation of the rôle of sexuality in religion. Brilliant as were his discoveries I believe that some of his assumptions as to the nature of the sex instinct and its relation to other primary impulses were remarkably erroneous. This being so one must treat with reserve his theories as to the part sex plays in religious observance and experience. Freud does not appear to have realized that such a thing as genuine religious experience can exist at all. His attitude to religion was full of sweeping generalizations determined by an inability to grasp the difference between, on the one hand, religiosity and religious observance under the coercion of fear, and, on the other, revealed religion. We must, however, defer discussion of these cardinal factors till we reach the section dealing with the relationship between the sexual and the self-assertive impulses.

V

FURTHER CRITICISMS OF THE FREUDIAN CONCEPT OF RELIGION

In the meantime are there any other arguments against the psychoanalytic concept of religion? Can a force which has existed throughout the ages from remotest antiquity be ascribed to the regular operation of neurotic factors? This is possible. Since man became aware of his separate identity he has always been insecure and his littleness and vulnerability in the face of the inscrutable machinations of fate have required the construction of comforting illusions. Let us grant that the predisposing insecurity has always existed. Let us admit the constant repetition of fear and guilt in the genesis of those psychiatric reactions which have encouraged the formation of religious systems. But why the persistence throughout aeons of time of a succession of father-figures involving the conception of God? Freud would say that the relationship with the human father always provides the material for the fabrication of God the Father. But how postulate the establishment of a long tradition of father-figures from one generation to another? The Freudian can answer this by saying that in every generation there are many so constituted as to offer themselves as ambassadors for father-figures in order to coerce others by means of theological systems of dogma. A priesthood so established, and so continued down the ages, could regularly solve its own problems of insecurity by the well-known mechanism of establishing power over others. But the nations for centuries have had alternative father-figures. As well as God the Father there was the father-figure of the king. The two father-figures have persisted together and an attempt to fuse their functions is exemplified by the doctrine of the divine right of kings.

For the most part the kings have gone but the idea of God the Father persists. The Freudian can argue that naturally alternative father-figures exist but one is bound to admit that there is something peculiarly tenacious in the God the Father idea. It must be admitted by the most agnostic that the conception of God has a peculiarly firm hold on the hearts and minds of men. The psychoanalytic arguments for the illusory nature of this concept may be regarded as convincing in the age and civilization we live in. Can they be applied with confidence to explain what has existed through so many different epochs and degrees of civilization? Even in our own day the Freudian doctrines as to the origins of religion are only applicable to our continent, to the civilizations derived from it and possibly to the religious systems which share with Freud a Semitic origin. They are of no help at all in explaining the religion of the millions who practice the Hindu and Buddhist faiths. There can be no Freudian mechanisms of guilt and atonement in religions where there are no father-figures and where God is not conceived of as a personal being. After all, we must remember that Christians have been good enough to describe Buddhism as a form of atheism. This disregard of the nature of religions infinitely older than Christianity and, possibly, even than the Hebrew faith is a remarkable and vital weakness of the Freudian system.

The trouble with the Freudian views on religion is that while they are undoubtedly impressive they are also a shade mechanical. They sound, indeed, a little like the more immovable concepts of reactionary theology. Shall we content ourselves by saying that man seems to have a persistent need of the idea of God? This does not really solve the problem for us. Man's needs are a poor guide and too often his worst illusions are fabricated in response to his direct needs. Such an argument serves only to support analytical theory. The real answer to Freud is three-fold. Firstly the recorded experience of the mystics is against the theory that religion is an illusion based on psychological abnormality. Secondly Freud's views of religion are only tenable in relation to the Jewish conception of a personal God and to the Christian conception of God as far as it is rooted in Judaism. Thirdly, while Freud's theories explain ingeniously man's need of God, they do not offer us any explanation of God's need of man.

VI

THE PHENOMENA OF MYSTICISM

We will deal first with the experience of the mystics. By this latter term I mean those whose religious approach is not through creeds and systems of belief but who either receive direct enlightenment or seek, by different means, such as prayer, fasting and meditation, direct experience of the presence of God. The first important point to be made is that the phenomena which accompany religious experience are remarkably constant. The experience of Henry Vaughan, described in his poem 'The World', is quite typical.

'I saw Eternity the other night
Like a great ring of pure and endless light,
All calm, as it was bright;
And round beneath it, Time, in hours, days, years,
Driv'n by the spheres,
Like a vast shadow mov'd, in which the world
And all her train were hurl'd.'

Now it is perfectly easy to dismiss this description as purely poetic and metaphorical. The fact remains that the ring of endless light is a very constant phenomenon in mystical experience. The light is almost always white. The sense of the uniformity of time as a timeless whole is also a regular feature of such experience. The mystic feels immortality not as something infinitely and mathematically extended but as something implied in the instant in which it is perceived. He feels free of the burden of himself, to be non-existent in terms of personality, and yet to exist as never before. In his state of being merged with God he feels himself to be beyond good and evil. Whatever emotions he has felt as he moved towards his revelation, in the moments in which he actually experiences it he is endowed with an indescribable sense of peace and an unshakeable conviction of the reality of his experience.

When reviewed on paper, there is nothing dramatic about the signs and symptoms of mystical experience. They are, indeed, embarrassingly simple to the point of naiveté. To those for whom truth must be intellectually or mathematically demonstrable they must carry little or no conviction. They can only be appreciated to the full by those for whom reality is an experience which carries its own meaning. But even to those for whom truth is essentially based on the faculty of reason there are one or two points to be noticed. Firstly, while the language of the mystic in pursuit of his goal is florid, sometimes stifling in its imagery and infinitely variable, the descriptions of the final achievement of reality are expressed in more limited terms which recur very constantly whatever the nationality or race of the mystic or whatever the age he lived in. The psychological experiences through which the individual passes in his pursuit of reality are multitudinous. They depend inevitably on his temperament, his cultural and social background and his epoch. The fact that the description of the transcendental experience itself is so relatively constant provides some indication of its reality.

VII

THE DISTINCTION BETWEEN MYSTICISM AND PSYCHIATRIC DISEASE

Now it can be argued that the signs and symptoms of mysticism are merely hallucinatory and that the mystic's unshakeable conviction of the reality of his experience is delusional. This, however, would imply that the mystical state is a mental illness in which the signs and symptoms exhibit a constancy unknown in any other psychiatric illness. In most varieties of schizophrenia hallucinations and delusions occur but these are of limitless variety. In mania the patient may suffer from delusions of grandeur but these latter have no constant content. The same applies to the grandiose delusions in general paralysis of the insane, while in melancholia there is a tendency to delusions as to bodily function but the nature of these latter is infinitely variable.

It is interesting that the mental illness where the delusional content is most constant is delirium tremens. This is a disease associated with excessive intake of alcohol or which is sometimes precipitated by its sudden withdrawal from a patient addicted to large quantities. It is popularly believed that hallucinations in which the patient sees rats and insects are common in this condition. This tradition is quite correct in that this type of hallucination does occur with quite significant frequency. In relation to the theme we are discussing this phenomenon is interesting. It has been said that every drug addict—and alcohol is the most common drug accessible to man—is a potential mystic. Certainly man has used alcohol since the beginnings of civilization. Ever since he developed an integrated personality he has sought to escape from it. Over the centuries alcohol has been the most readily available means enabling him to dissipate his sense of himself as a separate and isolated entity.

But the main point in diagnosing mystical experience from psychosis is the simple test of social usefulness. The mystic is transformed for the better by his experience. The psychotic is temporarily or permanently a social and personal failure. Is there any evidence that psychosis enhances the worth and expands the constructive potentialities of the individual? The question answers itself. The very fact that a large proportion of patients with mental illnesses are incarcerated in hospitals where nothing is required of them is adequate proof of what little a psychosis presents to the patient in the way of practical benefits.

It is possible from prejudice or misconception to diagnose St Francis, St Ignatius Loyola and John Wesley as mad, but it is difficult to know from what form of insanity they suffered. Access to mental hospitals at the present day will not result in the discovery of similar types, even of lesser calibre. The mental patient is not in the habit of producing religious and philosophical truths which change radically the outlook of his fellows. Any number of would-be philosophers and prophets are to be found in the population of any large mental hospital. But the acid test, in relation to our immediate argument, is that these cases have little or nothing of value to communicate except to the psychiatrist in search of material. Indeed, the cardinal difference between the true mystic and the mental hospital prophet is simply that the former has, either actually or potentially, an immense social usefulness, whereas the latter is essentially a social failure.

VIII

ART AND PSYCHIATRIC DISORDER

It is a common misconception that in the spheres of art and philosophy there is evidence that constructive work of the highest value can be produced by those afflicted with mental disorder. I raise this question here because art, like religious feeling, is an experience of reality and because philosophy is at least a search, though often a hobbling and fruitless one, dedicated to the same aim. The old, familiar argument runs that genius is allied to insanity. Of all the feats of popular mythology this is among the most ridiculous. It is a largely modern vulgarism arising from a decadent conception of democracy which assumes that the mediocre is inevitably the normal. Certainly Van Gogh takes some explaining away. During certain epochs of life he was definitely psychotic. But were these periods the most fruitful of his career even allowing for the extraordinary number of pictures he produced in the mental hospital at St Remy? It is nevertheless extremely rare for an individual to produce anything of tangible, let alone of transcendental, value in the throes of a mental illness.

Nietzsche is regarded by some as the greatest philosopher of the last century. He died in a mental hospital. In my view he was psychiatrically abnormal for years but there is no evidence whatever that during the time he was writing his books he was abnormal to the degree of mental illness.

Work of great value has been achieved by a very small minority prone to psychotic disorders but for the most part this has been accomplished in intervals between the outbreaks of mental illness. The poet Cowper is a case in point. So far as one can ascertain he was subject to attacks of melancholia. In this connection it should be remembered that the basic symptom of this illness is severe depression. Now this latter phenomenon also occurs very frequently in ordinary neurotic illness. In considering such cases, occurring before the advent of modern psychiatry, we should make allowance for the possibility that some severe depressive conditions burdened with the label of melancholia were in actual fact not mental but neurotic disturbances.

It should also be remembered that any new form of art or system of thought not understood by the majority is commonly regarded as a product of insanity. This particular vice is almost certainly more prevalent in modern democracy than in the more privileged societies which preceded it. In the age of the common man the supernormal will always be more indictable than the subnormal. The latter can be pitied but the former must of necessity be hated. After all, to see things in their intrinsic reality and as others do not see them, is a form of cheating which is hardly tolerable in an age of equal shares of pearls for swine.

Against the small number of artists and thinkers with a history of psychosis there is to be set the enormous majority not similarly afflicted. This may be news to those who consider that genius and insanity are closely allied. But if you start from the assumption that genius is insanity then of course your argument is irrefutable.

Quite recently I have been studying advertisements for a new variety of tranquillisers. These advertisements are distinguished by an aura of tabloid culture suitably diluted with the prevailing materialism. Each is accompanied by the picture of a great man and what is presumed to be an appropriate quotation from his works. Comment is provided by excerpts from a book called the Great Abnormals. This work is presumably out of date but possibly still in print. It is instructive to weigh the evidence offered for the insanity of Mozart. The latter confessed that his music 'was not the result of his personal will or striving, but that it came to him like dreams.' The feeling that inspiration arises outside the personality and is imposed on the individual without the co-operation of his will is an experience common to many artists of the first rank. After all, we say that inspiration comes and not that we have made it. To quote this as evidence of psychosis is to misunderstand completely the nature of artistic inspiration. If we accept the view that the feeling of inspiration from without is a sign of grave psychiatric disturbance then, this experience being so common, we are committed to the view that the mental processes behind much, if not all, of our greatest art are psychotic. I do not think even this age, in which the desire to debunk has become an obsession, is prepared to go as far as that.

If the phenomena associated with mystical experience are not to be regarded as the signs and symptoms of mental illness, can they be explained as neurotic in origin? The only neurosis which could possibly be considered in this connection is hysteria. But in this latter condition, far from the symptoms being simple and clean cut, they are infinitely more variable than those observed in the anxiety and obsessional neuroses and their variety is indeed almost limitless. All manner of pains, sensations, pseudo-pareses and states of local anaesthesia can occur as well as numerous other symptoms not classifiable under the afore-mentioned headings. There can be no doubt that many cases falsely regarded as examples of mystical experience originate in hysteria or are contaminated by it, but the difference between hysterical conditions and true states of mysticism is cardinal.

In distinguishing between mystical experience and psychoses we used as criteria the effect of each on the capacity for social and productive effort. If we apply the same criteria in distinguishing between hysteria and mysticism we will obtain similar results. The form of hysteria most likely to be confused with mystical experience has often a schizoid background. The hysterical symptoms are merely a deceptive top-dressing for an essentially psychotic disturbance. Of all forms of neurosis profound hysteria is the least socially adaptable, the least productive and the most unrewarding from the point of view of treatment. This applies whether or no the symptoms of hysteria are accompanied by a schizoid background. Hysterics of this nature show none of the steadfastness and dedication which characterises the mystic. They may exhibit *la belle indifference* of those who have solved their problem by the evasion of reality. The mystic, on the other hand, lives in his experience of reality and his efforts are enriched by it.

The cure of any neurosis is slow and even then the patient is notoriously prone to relapses. The mystic's passage, after the process of conviction, into calmer waters is by comparison rapid. His liability to relapse is small. This factor in prognosis is very important in the differential diagnosis between mysticism and neurotic states.

Again, hysteria is essentially an escape from reality, whereas mystical experience is a conviction of it. In addition, the hysteric is highly suggestible and his symptoms are essentially produced by suggestion. The true mystic is less than all others suggestible to human influences. The diminished emphasis he places on the importance of his own personality renders the latter less vulnerable to influences conducive to disease. Finally, the hysterical reaction is essentially a plea to others and a craving for affection or attention. The mystic is at the opposite pole. He does not use his personality as a magnet to attract the attention of his fellows. He offers it without reservation to God, the Absolute or what he conceives to be a universal spirit.

But perhaps the conviction of truth implicit in mystical experience is the most important distinguishing factor between it and the psychiatric states with which it might conceivably be confused. It is characteristic that nothing can shake the mystic's belief in the reality of his experience. Now it can be argued that the psychotic patient cannot be reasoned out of his delusions and this is indeed incontrovertible because a delusion is essentially something the individual holds to be true in spite of all reasonable proof to the contrary. But the psychotic patient is in almost all cases impeded or even paralysed as a functioning unit. The potentialities of the mystic are enhanced by the experience he has undergone. Even if he persists in, or embraces, a monastic existence, he continues to function as an integrated being and most often on a higher plane than formerly. Again, it should be remembered that the number of individuals who have undergone mystical experience and who lead afterwards a secluded life is probably much smaller than those who engage in more active forms of existence. It is a fallacy to regard the mystic as essentially shut off from the world. Certainly in his search for reality it is common for him to spend long hours in contemplation. On the other hand, once he has experienced the conviction of the peace of God he very often resumes earlier and non-contemplative habits of life but with the difference that, whereas formerly he functioned as a separate entity, he now does so as an instrument of something higher, wider and deeper than himself.

It is characteristic of some mystics that they speak little of their experiences. The materialist may argue that this is analogous to the type of paranoid patient who ceases to disclose his delusions because he realizes that, however real they are to him, they are unacceptable to the majority. But such a patient maintains a characteristically paranoid attitude even though he has ceased to express his delusions. He is very often guarded, hostile, abnormally suspicious and employs a form of pseudo-brilliant argumentation which is too good to be true. After all, many human beings argue with greater facility the worse their case. The mystic, on the other hand, may be loath to define his experience because he knows it to be inexpressible. There is no real nomenclature for feeling. When we realize how inadequate are the descriptions of human love even in great literature, it is not surprising that the mystic should not endeavour to express what is even more ineffable. Again, those who have undergone mystical revelations are not to be accused of diffidence or lack of moral courage if they feel that what they know is simply not understandable by those not like-minded or who have not undergone similar experiences. I remember a healthy, athletic and well-balanced woman who admitted to a mystical experience but said she saw no point in discussing its nature. When she saw that I had a genuine and, I hope, unsensational interest in the subject, she disclosed to me the nature of what I feel sure was a genuine mystical experience. This attitude of mind exemplifies the great truth of religious experience that those who say don't know and those who know don't say.

But is the mystic's conviction of reality enough of itself to convince us as to the reality of his experience? After all, the delusional patient's unshakeable belief in his delusions is held with equal tenacity. The answer surely lies in the effect of such a conviction on the life of the individual concerned. The history of religion is full of examples of those who, convinced of the reality of their mystic experiences, have led lives which must be regarded as unusually constructive even according to the standards of the most sceptical.

It should also be remembered that mystics are not to be found only in those canonized or remembered with reverence by the religious sects to which they have belonged. Such mystics as we know by name are those of the articulate variety whose writings or sayings are still preserved. It is of the very nature of mystical experience that those who have known it, however articulate they may have been before the actual experience itself, tend afterwards to silence, having reached the conviction that truth is deeper than words. This being so, it is probably safe to assume that the number of mystics who have gone humbly about their daily duties without leaving for mankind any special communication, is vastly greater than those who have committed their convictions to paper or who have preached a gospel particularly associated with their name. It should also be remembered that many mystics have distinguished themselves as men of action. Naturally a number of these have been engaged in religious activities. John Wesley and some of the great Quakers were not only mystics but actively employed in preaching and organization. Again, the mystic as man of action is found operating not solely in the sphere of religion. The number of great soldiers who have with some justification regarded themselves as instruments of God is by no means inconsiderable. The case of Henry Vaughan, whose great mystical poem has already been quoted, is of considerable interest. Vaughan ceased to write poetry at an early age and worked for the greater part of his life as a doctor in Wales. It is facile to assume that he ceased to write poetry because he was disappointed at its reception, because the wells of inspiration had run dry, or because the troubled times in which he lived were unsuitable for composition. It is perfectly possible that, having experienced the reality celebrated in his poems, he found no further need to express himself through this medium, but reverted to more mundane ways of living, but with a new outlook and as a divine instrument.

IX

FREUDIAN THEORY AND OTHER WORLD RELIGIONS

It is now necessary to deal with the second of our three main objections to the Freudian interpretation of religion. This latter is only tenable in relation to the concept of a personal God and, moreover, to a God conceived of in man's image. It is a feat of psychological gymnastics beyond the capacity of most to feel guilt in relation to a universal spirit pervading all things. It is easy to produce guilt reactions in relation to a God conceived of as an ever watchful father endowed with the capacity to bless or to punish. In Buddhism and Hinduism God is not endowed with the personal qualities bestowed on Him in Jewish and Christian belief. He is conceived of as a spirit infiltrating all things and to which all things will return. It cannot be disputed that the neuroses, which are among the major curses of our Western civilization, are of infinitely smaller incidence against a Buddhist or Hindu background.

Freud has argued that our sense of guilt is part of the basis structure of religion. Many Christian ecclesiastics, who deplore his influence, are at least at one with him in their insistence that guilt is part of the proper equipment of the Christian. We are often encouraged by eminent divines to develop this apparently desirable quality. (It is surely not irrelevant at this juncture to suggest that Christ came to take away the sins of the world). And as well as this sense of guilt we have the passion to atone which derives from it and which manifests itself in the obsessional ritual of religious observance. Again, it is less easy to atone to an invisible, timeless, all-pervading spirit than it is to a separate entity, be the latter the personal God of the Christian or the animistic Gods of thunder and lightning. The savage placating his deity with offerings of food or animals, the Christian and the Jew with their complicated rituals, are each examples of the desire to atone to separate-entity Gods. Ritual, too, occurs in the two great religions of the Far East but in their purer forms it plays a small part compared with its rôle in Christianity and Judaism and there are forms of Buddhism in which ritual plays no part whatever. (It cannot be denied that in places Buddhism appears to have developed a complex ceremonial which, in our eyes, would seem, in some particulars, to stand in close relation to primitive superstition. But who are we to criticise?) Certainly ritual has never been regarded as so near to the core of Buddhism and Hinduism as the spiritual techniques, so little developed in the West, which enable the devoté to make contact with the timeless and formless God Who is everywhere and within him also.

It is commonly held that Christianity has its philosophical, as apart from its divine, origins in Hellenism and Judaism. It is often argued that the great contribution of Judaism is monotheism. This view seems to me parochial. The concept of one God as a spirit infusing all things has been an essential feature of Buddhism and Hinduism for centuries before the advent of Christianity. It probably predates the acceptance of monotheism as a cardinal tenet of the Jewish faith.

As I have said before, Christian ecclesiastics have been loath to admit that the Universal Spirit in Buddhism and Hinduism is to be regarded as God, and have even gone so far as to describe these religions as atheistic. It is quite common to find them referred to by Christian priests and ministers as not religions but philosophical systems. The explanation of this attitude is that such Christian ecclesiastics cannot conceive of God as anything other than a person. To them devotion to a deity in impersonal form does not qualify for the description of monotheism.

Monotheism in the Western World certainly has its origins in Judaism. Whether or no the concept of a universal spirit in Eastern religions pre-dates or post-dates the appearance of monotheism in the West and Middle East is not of great moment. The important fact is that the conception of a single spirit in the Far Eastern religions was not derived from Judaism and did not exhibit the same characteristics as the Jewish version of this radical principle.

The doctrine of monotheism is usually regarded by theologians as an immense step forward in the spiritual evolution of the human species. The importance of this particular advance can be exaggerated. Its value as food for the soul of man must necessarily depend on its nature. It is difficult for many to find the Jehovah of the Old Testament consistently attractive. He appears to us in many guises but too often, in relation to ordinary human standards, his behaviour is vindictive, unforgiving and ruthless and his memory for insults inconveniently long. He exhibits too often the paranoid attitude of a dictator. In some of his moods he is the figurehead of Jewish nationalism. The Old Testament conception of the functions of his son, the Messiah, was not free from the tinge of imperialism. He would come to rule the kingdoms of the earth as the leader of a dominant Jewish race and in so doing would avenge the tribulations and captivities of his people. It is a little naïve to regard this conception of a single god as a considerable advance on the religious beliefs of Hellenism. For long periods during what is called the heroic age of Greece the deities worshipped were symbols of natural forces such as Jupiter or Zeus or heroes translated to a higher sphere and conducting their exploits on a vaster scale. It was often noticeable that following their translation to heaven the morals of the heroes suffered a disastrous decline. To some there may be little to choose between the vivacious and amoral Gods of the Greeks and the god of the

Old Testament. But the later ages of Greek culture saw the contributions of Plato and other philosophers to our conception of the nature of God. It is this contribution to which we refer when we speak of Christianity having, in part, its philosophical foundations in Hellenism. But Greek thought had not before the advent of Christianity cohered into an organized faith with monotheism as one of its guiding principles. It is possible that this idea may have been a central belief in some of the esoteric faiths practised in Greece in the last centuries before the advent of Christ, but this is no more than conjecture.

With the advent of Christianity the nature of the Old Testament god was considerably amended. God was now something more than periodically amiable and became the loving father Who sent His Son to redeem the world. Again, moulded by the new influence which softened the human heart, man recreated God in his own image. At the same time God retained His right as the supreme arbiter of the world to judge and, if necessary, to punish sinners. In the main Christianity preserved the Jewish conception of God as a supreme being rather than an influence. It is somewhat doubtful as to what extent this belief was widespread among early Christians. Nevertheless, the doctrine of the Holy Trinity, which for centuries has been one of the main buttresses of the Christian faith, suggests that on the whole the belief in God as a personal being has been steadily maintained. The mere fact that so much theological study has been expended in differentiating between the Father, the Son and the Holy Spirit suggests that the idea of a personal God has, though challenged by some, remained relatively unshaken throughout the ages.

X

NEUROSIS AND THE CONCEPTION OF A PERSONAL GOD

Freud has demonstrated how the child's reactions to his earthly father and to his Heavenly Father are closely related to each other. The love and fear of the child for his father are reflected in his love and fear of God. God is a supreme power and the child's attitude towards Him is coloured by his own experiences of his earthly father as the lord of his circumscribed world. We may teach that God is love but the child's conception of God is essentially that of a watchful being, loving perhaps, but noting his transgressions, perhaps not with anger, perhaps only with sorrow. But God is necessarily depicted as a personal being with personal reactions. It is the child's good fortune if he grow up in a house where God is hurt by his transgressions rather than moved to retribution. The psychological damage he experiences is probably less. But suppose instead of the idea of God as a personal being He is conceived of as an universal influence? How then does the child develop the guilt reactions and the obsessional desires to atone which Freud describes, and with reason, as the basis of so much religious observance? It can be argued that it is beyond the capacity of the child to conceive of God in anything other than personal form. This may be so, for the Western child, saturated in an atmosphere where God is conceived of as a personal entity and bearing within his mind the ancestral memory of such a belief. But the conception of God as an all-pervading spirit offers no difficulty to millions of beings, whether they be children or adults, who exist in Buddhist and Hindu communities.

It can be argued that one labours too much the Christian concept of God as some form of supreme personality. It can be said with justification that in Christianity God is conceived of as in all things. This latter view may be accepted by a proportion of Christians but I think it is only actually *felt* by a still smaller proportion. Here again the belief in God as within us and in everything is of limited development compared with its incidence in the Far Eastern religions. The Christian refers to the Holy Spirit operating within him. This is by no means the same as being part of an all-pervading and limitless God. The Holy Spirit is essentially conceived of as a gift of the Father. The spirit is an influence, the Father remains a being. It is also of great significance that the Christian saint is so often indivisible with Christ, not God. St Thérèse of Lisieux regarded herself as one with Jesus. Such a condition does not represent a mere difference in degree from the Eastern mystic's identification with the Infinite. The difference is essentially one of kind. The Western mystic may be as wholly lost in Christ as the Eastern in the universal spirit, but Christ, again, is essentially something sent by God. He is, in fact, the supreme gift of the Supreme Being. Where the identification is complete the result will be the same in the case of the Western Christian absorbed in Christ and in that of the Eastern merged with the Infinite. But for the less ardent and less successful aspirant seeking to be merged in Christ the problem is much more difficult because he is essentially seeking identification with something secondary to, and dependent on, the love and mercy of a Supreme Being conceived of as a person.

If we accept Freud's theories we are bound to acknowledge that the personal nature of God is a factor of immense importance in introducing neurotic factors into the groundwork of Western religion.

In studying the subject of neurosis and religion we should be careful to distinguish between cause and effect. Much organized religion is based, in part at any rate, on neurotic factors. This is not to say that the practitioners of such religions are conspicuously neurotic, according to Western standards. The Roman faith would, according to Freud, afford us probably the best example of a creed having its origins in neurosis. The ritual and the repetitive prayers are not only based on obsessional tendencies but are themselves obsessional in nature. The sense of guilt, the impulse to atone and the technique of atonement can be regarded as neurotic mechanisms. Yet on the whole Roman Catholics are less neurotic than their Protestant brethren. The neurotic tendency is expressed in the mechanism of the religion and less is available for the production of neurotic symptoms falling into the usual psychiatric categories. But this is by no means the whole truth. The Roman confessional is an excellent safety valve for incipient neurosis. In addition, the God of the Roman Catholic is in these days relatively goodnatured compared with the God of the Noncomformist. He is more easy to placate by the atoning rituals provided. It cannot be doubted that the ritual of Roman catholicism absorbs and renders innocuous a good deal of potential neurosis among its adherents. This is proved by the fact that the obsessional neurosis, so specifically concerned with ritualistic acts and thoughts, is far less common among Roman Catholics than Protestants.

On the other hand the nature of a religion can prove

specially conducive to neurosis. This is true of the more puritanical Protestant faiths. The more harsh and inhibiting the faith, the more its God is concerned with retribution and hell fire, the more neurosis is to be expected among its adherents. This is particularly true of such sects as the Plymouth Brethren, Baptists. Methodists and Presbyterians are also on the whole more prone to neurotic disturbance than their Roman confrères.

XI

THE PERSISTENCE OF JUDAISM IN CHRISTIANITY

We have seen that the concept of a personal God as distinct from a universal spirit is conducive to the production of neurotic factors in the groundwork of religion. Where God is endowed with paranoid and revengeful tendencies it is possible for suppressed resentment to be engendered in the minds and hearts of those who regard themselves as believers. Even where God is considered more merciful than the Jehovah of the Old Testament the doctrine of punishment for sin still endows Him with powers which, to the individual in secret revolt, are both undesirable and arbitrary. It is possible that anti-Semitism is, in part, a veiled expression of resentment for Jehovah. The person of anti-Semitic tendencies is enabled to expend his hate on the so-called chosen people without enduring the discomforts of a direct defiance of God. I do not think anti-Semitism to the degree of active racial intolerance is to be explained entirely by the fact that in some countries many Jews are rich and hold positions of power to a degree excessive for a racial minority. It is said that resentment of them is increased because they retain their faith and traditions and are not wholly absorbed in the background of the country in which they are living. I doubt if these suppositions are tenable. Many *are* absorbed and many Jews have a facile intelligence which aids rather than impedes the process of absorption. Besides, anti-Semitism is also prevalent in communities where the vast majority of Jews are of the poorer classes, as in pre-war Poland. In England we have surely surrendered more positions of wealth and importance to the Celtic fringe, if we, for the purposes of this argument regard the Scots as Celts, than we have to the Jews, yet there is little evidence of anti-Celtic feeling among us. The persistence and, in certain countries, the ferocity of anti-Semitism, cannot wholly be attributed to the fact that the masses in time of hardship resent the apparent welfare of people of a different race. This sort of reaction is natural in any country with a foreign population in times of stress. In Germany many of the Jews who were murdered had been domiciled for so long in that country that they could not be considered foreign. The phenomenon of anti-Semitism bears all the marks of a long-standing and deep-seated malady. The massacre of the Jews in the last war was unexampled in modern history. One might have thought that in the revulsion from it anti-Semitism would have become almost extinct. So far as one can ascertain it seems to be increasing again in Poland and Russia.

Indeed there is still much to regret in the legacy of Judaism which persists in Christianity. What of the sabbatarianism of the rigid Presbyterian? Christ declared that the Sabbath was made for man and not man for the Sabbath, yet in this matter the whole-hearted Presbyterian sides with the Jewish ecclesiastics who interrogated Christ rather than with Christ Himself. Consider the example of the Lord's Day Observance Society. This steadfast and curious organization has in recent years interfered considerably in the social life of this country. Its adherents apparently see no contradiction in the fact that they take the name of the Lord in vain in contravening His principles. Till recently the principal Christian churches still adhered to the Jewish edict that women's heads should be covered in church. The mutilating operation of circumcism is still practised on Christian children for reasons said to be sanitary but which are in fact mythological. There is much in Nietzsche's contention that a Christian is merely a kind of Protestant Jew.

The facts quoted above are extreme examples of the persistence in our own time of the principles of Judaism in the Christian faith. In relation to our thesis they are probably of less importance than the continuance in our time of the idea of God as the supreme judge with the power to reward or to condemn eternally. Can it be that Freud's theories were influenced by the fact that he himself was a Jew?

We have the evidence of Freud himself that in his early

youth he was deeply concerned about his racial origins. His father told him how on one occasion he was affronted by some ebullient Teuton. Freud admits that he was shocked and contemptuous that his father had not retaliated appropriately. This is the sort of incident which, given other related circumstances, Freud would have considered of importance in the analysis of his patients. In suggesting that religion as a whole was an illusion he was also demolishing the faith of his fathers. In undermining the religion of his race he was destroying the strongest force which held it together. In so doing he was removing also the greatest justification for its ostracism and, incidentally, was solving his own problem.

XII

EVALUATION OF FREUD

Had Freud been born a Buddhist he might still have established the broad principles of psychoanalytical theory and possibly with still greater accuracy but he could not have entertained the views on religion which he expressed in the Future of an Illusion. The individual with the seeds of rebellion within him cannot react effectively against a universal spirit within himself as well as in time and space. Moreover there is relatively little incitement to revolt against religious and philosophical systems which, like Hinduism and Buddhism, insist that the fate of man is so much in his own hands and not to be decided by the judgements of a watchful God. It is significant that Hindu and Buddhist communities, while they may contain many who are indifferent to the influence of their religion, do not produce the militant atheists and anit-clericals who are such a distinctive feature of the European scene. As the East becomes Westernised this deplorable deficiency should be suitably amended.

Like the vast majority of mankind, Freud was vulnerable in that his powers of reasoning could be vitiated by hidden resentments and emotional factors over which he had inadequate control. The fact that he was the father of psychoanalysis provides no reason to credit him with the fullest insight into the motives which governed his own life. It is possible that only a neurotic could have produced the brilliant, fertile but sometimes fallacious theories of psychoanalysis. His vulnerability is revealed in his remarkably naïve veneration for what he called science. He appears to have been completely honest, at the conscious level. No one can ask more of a man than that. But perhaps he could not appreciate to the full the degree to which his anti-religious attitude was as much determined by neurotic factors as the religious preoccupations of others. That he was a great man cannot be denied. That he was fitted to speak with authority on the subject of religion is open to question. He seems never to have realized, against the evidence of centuries, that there is a reality of religious experience apart from the psychopathological makeshift of much organized religion.

XIII

RELIGION WITHOUT POWER

We have seen how Freud's theories are based on man's need of God. The orthodox practitioner of religion for whom Freud's theories are anathema would, however, make the same statement as to the origin of his own beliefs. The difference is that Freud insists that man's needs are an insecure guide and that what he erects from them is an illusion. But what if religion were based partly on God's need of man? If this were so religion, even conceived of in terms of psychoanalytic theory, would not be dependent on father-figures nor its ritual on a sense of guilt and the desire to atone. We cannot conceive of God as afflicted with a sense of guilt in relation to man. We cannot, here in the West at any rate, think of Him as supporting Himself on an infinite number of son-figures. If we regard God as a supreme being, with some of the attributes of personality, we are endowing Him with the attributes of power. If we consider that God, too, may need us as we Him then we are denying Him His status as all-powerful. As soon as we do this we threaten the whole foundations of the Freudian theory of religion. We do not organize rituals of atonement to gods of limited power. We do not offer penances to gods whom we know to be incapable of extracting them. It may be argued that we do not worship to placate God but I think such arguments flatter us unduly. If we adopt this flattering view of ourselves we are flying in the face of a great deal of the ecclesiastical opinion which seeks to guide us. Priests and ministers of puritanical inclination, be they Scottish Presbyterians or Irish Roman Catholics, still threaten us, sometimes with hell fire, more often with other less highly-coloured species of damnation. From the mildest ecclesiastics we hear of the horrors of being excluded from God's presence. This is well enough if it is made clear that the act of exclusion is originated by us. It must be admitted that this latter view is encountered often enough among the more enlightened clergy but I cannot think that these constitute a majority. It would not be in human nature if they did. If we are tempted to criticize the priesthood as a whole we must remember that it is recruited from fallible humans and must therefore be imperfect.

We may say that when we ask forgiveness of God it is not from fear but because we have hurt Him by our transgressions. This relatively refined attitude is, indeed, adopted in many Christian homes. The child is often instructed that by his transgressions he has wounded a Loving Father who sent His son to save us. But as soon as we credit God with the capacity to forgive we endow him with supreme power. The capacity to forgive implies that He has also the capacity either to punish or not to forgive and that He has abstained from the employment of this power in our particular case. On the whole we must admit that we remain faithful to the liturgy in attributing to God all Might, Majesty, Dominion and Power.

Now is there any justification for the belief that God is not all-powerful and is to some degree dependent on us? The idea has been expressed by William James, who asked if God Himself might not acquire strength from our fidelity. Meister Eckhardt had similar views. Much Albigensian doctrine supported this attitude. The Albigensians could not accept that Christ was God Incarnate. They argued that it was impossible for a divinity to inhabit anything so contaminated with sin as the human body. Similarly they denied that God created the world. The latter, to them, was so saturated in evil that it must have been created by the devil. Like the Manichean heresy, which was also rigorously persecuted, they believed that the universe was a balance between the forces of good and evil. In the end the good would triumph, God would reign and the devil himself be redeemed. All this implies a clear belief in the existence of God. It embodied, too, a heroic willingness to die in His Service. It also expresses with equal clarity the belief that God was by no means omnipotent. Indeed it asserts very positively that our existence on earth is a reverse for God in the battle between good and evil.

Though the Albigensians did not accept Christ as the Son of God they believed in a Holy Spirit. There is considerable evidence that this was regarded as female. This conception is of the greatest significance and has no analogies whatever with the worship of Mary as the Mother of Christ. Mary was the instrument through which an omnipotent God, by the agency of the Holy Spirit, created His Son to redeem the world. But to endow the Holy Spirit with female attributes is to go much further. To do so is to elevate the feminine virtues of love and mercy and to avoid their contamination with the principle of power symbolised by the male. We may argue that the Holy Spirit according to orthodox Christian doctrine is not necessarily conceived of as male. This may be so but the point is that it is not, as in Albigensian doctrine, specifically conceived of as female. In relation to religions based on conceptions of God the Father, a creed with a specifically female Holy Spirit represents a considerable abnegation of the power principle. This is what we might expect of a creed which denied the omnipotence of God.

The Albigensian faith, in regarding the world as the production of the devil, expressed a somewhat extreme limitation of the power of God. Other Christian creeds which deplore the wickedness of the world and the flesh are none the less convinced that God will intervene in His own good time. In general, the more the creed deplores the sinfulness of the world the more it is convinced that, when God does intervene, He will do so with great force and extract from us a heavy punishment for our sins. In Christianity we always conceive of God as ultimately intervening either on our behalf or to our detriment. But what of the religions where God does not intervene, where we go to Him rather than He to us, where salvation depends more exclusively on our own efforts and where salvation itself involves our being finally lost in universality and not translated into Heaven in virtue of His supreme power? The God of the Buddhist and Hindu is conceived of as a universal influence but certainly not as a powerful being. He will not, by His own intervention, establish His Kingdom in due time. He is timeless and in all things but in relation to our God He does not function as a personality nor does He bend circumstances to His will. He does not claim that we will sit in glory on His right hand. He offers us death in Him. As He is impersonal, so it is our reward to be freed of ourselves and to become impersonal as He is. In relation to such a God how is it possible to develop the guilt reactions and other manifestations which afflict the Christian haunted as much, and more, by the power of God as by His love?

The essense of true religion is to think and act for God's sake and not our own. When, with no thought of rewards or punishments, and with our minds freed from preoccupations with personality, we do what we do for the sake of God, we have ceased to regard Him as a supreme power. To live for His sake is to further His influence. If His influence can be furthered by our efforts His power cannot be regarded as supreme. Unless we conceive of Him as omnipotent we cannot develop towards Him the guilt and fear reactions which Freud alleges are at the basis of religion. Once again, in the face of a truly religious attitude, the Freudian theories are found to be inadequate.

In formulating his theories Freud cannot have considered adequately the religions of the Far East. Had he done so he would have realized that, however much his hypotheses were applicable to a great proportion of believers in the Western world, they could not apply to those religions which, taken together, are not only numerically greater than Christianity but which existed long before its advent.

From many points of view we may say that there is only one fundamental religion in the world. This religion has for its guiding principle the belief that God is everywhere and in all things and that our spiritual aim is to achieve Oneness with Him. Though we assert that the philosophical origins of Christianity are in Hellenism and Judaism we should consider it possible that it also derives from the Far Eastern religions. If we hold that the mystic, as apart from the orthodox believer, is near to the heart of the matter, we are bound to admit that the Christian mystic, in seeking the presence of God, is adopting an attitude similar to, if not identical with, those who in the Far East approach the Absolute through processes of meditation which, though not peculiar to them, are accounted as orthodox among them. It has even been stated that the years in Christ's life not accounted for in the Gospels were spent in the Far East and that He came in contact with Buddhist doctrines. This view is obviously more derived from a study of the analogies between the teachings of Christ and Buddha than from historical evidence. But the spiritual atmosphere of the gospel of St John draws close to that of the Far Eastern religions. It has been well said that in our religious life we are leaving behind the age of Paul and entering that of John. The interest in the Eastern religions is increasing greatly. I myself have observed this in patients who could not be described as of high culture or as being endowed with philosophic interests. What this means is that in the West people are moving away from religions based on immutable dogma to those founded on verifiable states of mind and feeling. God is, after all, not felt so much in the brain as in the heart and solar plexus. It is the intensely theological religions which are both based on neurosis and which produce it. If civilization continues, future Western religion will not be based so predominantly on so-called theological truths but on the truths of feeling and actual experience. We will either know God, in the same way as we know our mother or the village street, or we will not know Him at all. Freud appears to have been utterly incapable of appreciating that religious feeling can exist as a felt reality demanding no dogma for the proof of its validity. He elucidated brilliantly the emotional conflicts which are at the basis of such dogma. He could not believe that the whole feeling life of the individual could discover reality and its own religious truths. It is perhaps understandable that he should be uninfluenced by the evidence of the Christian mystics or that his disciples should regard them as pathological. That his theories should be inapplicable to the two great religions which account for so large a proportion of the world's population is less easy to condone.

We have seen that religion according to Freud is a mass obsessional neurosis. Now this latter malady is essentially the scourge of the individual with the driving and productive personality of which he is acutely aware. The aim of the obsessional, with his perfectionism and undue meticulousness, is to make a self-contained work of art of his own life. The obsessional neurotic is the apotheosis of Western Protestant man in all his conscientiousness, perfectionism and spiritual isolation. Now the Far Eastern religions demand a degree of abnegation of the personality almost impossible to attain in Western man. Such religions are neither based on the obsessional state nor are they productive of it. They cannot be considered as deriving from the origins which Freud attributes to religion as a whole.

XIV

SUMMARY OF THE FALLACIES IN THE PSYCHOANALYTIC EXPLANATION OF RELIGION

It might be objected that in considering the psychoanalytical view of religion I have considered too exclusively the theories of Freud. Certainly Jung has much to say on the subject of religion. His views are at variance with those of Freud. But it cannot be doubted that the principles of Freud provided the groundwork of psychoanalytical theory and also the original dissection of religion on analytic lines. In spite of Jung's additions to knowledge it cannot be claimed on his behalf that, except for the concept of the racial unconscious, he outlined any of the fundamental mechanisms of mind as modern psychiatry understands them. The doctrine of the unconscious, the mechanisms of repression and sublimation, and the mode of origin of phobias and obsessions are all the work of Freud. If one speaks of the psychoanalytical view of religion one is referring, for all but the purist, to the teaching of the Viennese master. For the purpose of this thesis one is therefore justified in confining oneself to the latter's basic theories.

I think it is fair in summarising to say that the psychoanalytic view of religion cannot be regarded as proved. It applies, and often with unerring brilliance, to much of the structure of organized religion in Western civilization. I imagine that its application to the Jewish religion is valid to at least the same degree but my knowledge of this faith is insufficient to enable me to dogmatize. Any organized religion is tinged with all manner of ancestral, traditional and racial theories and I think we are wiser if we speak with something less than assurance of those which are not our own. But even within the orbit of our Western faiths Freud is an uncertain guide. His explanations apply to those for whom religion is a traditional and comforting inheritance which they accept without much questioning as to its nature and without much self-analysis. His theories also account for the preoccupations and observances of those for whom organized religion is an efficient solution for their emotional problems. But all this is merely begging the question. Such types as the above are those for whom religion is a consolation but who are, in themselves, essentially irreligious. It may even be that churches serve their best purpose as reminders to the naturally unspiritual that higher values exist. What Freud is really saying is that religion is based on insecurity because it is for the insecure. His hypothesis does not explain the reactions of those who either within or without the confines of religion are seeking the presence of God and to achieve One-ness with Him. Naturally, to the whole-hearted Freudian, the more truly religious the person the more he is the victim of illusion. The reader must weigh the evidence for himself. At the same time one should warn him to beware of all intellectual systems which explain all things too neatly. The Freudian hypothesis claims almost a papal infallibility on behalf of its scientific derivations. The human mind is not a computing machine and mathematics is, after all, not a form of truth but the ultimate abstraction.

Finally, there is one other important weakness in the Freudian system and that is that it never makes adequate allowance for the effect on the individual of the prevailing sociological and philosophical climate. Forty years ago general paralytics commonly exhibited a grandiose and fatuously happy phase in which they conducted themselves as though they were the lords of creation. This desirable condition was followed traditionally by a less fortunate set of circumstances in which the patient was described as dirty, demented and damned. In the last four decades the grandiose phase has been disappearing and humanity has had to satisfy itself with the poor bargain of depression and increasing dementia. Again, in the years since the war the number of cases of severe non-psychotic depression has increased enormously. Can one brush aside lightly the suggestion that the dolorous and crucial circumstances in which we live are related to the increase in the number of depressive illnesses and to the emphasis on depressive factors in others? Freud insisted quite rightly that the turmoils within man create the climate in which he lives but did he make sufficient allowance for the effect on man of the impact of the total atmosphere so created? I mention this factor especially in relation to his observations on religion. It cannot be denied that he failed to see that while the climate of orthodox Christianity may be especially conducive to neurosis that of the Far Eastern religions has no analogous effect. We will consider further the special question of Christianity in relation to neurosis in the next section.

PART TWO

Christianity and Neurosis

I

THE SPECIAL ROLE OF CHRISTIANITY IN THE INDUCTION OF NEUROSIS

Though I have argued that Freud's views on religion are too all-inclusive and on the whole fallacious, I have not denied that they enlighten us considerably as to the origins of a great deal of organised religion. If neurosis enters considerably into the fabric of religion it will not be surprising to discover that religion itself is capable of inducing neurotic reactions. In this section we will consider whether Christianity is especially conducive to these morbid responses.

II

THE DOCTRINE OF THE RESURRECTION

We cannot deny that there is more neurosis in Christian communities than in the other world religions. I have dealt with this more fully in another work.[1] In comparison with the East, Western culture not only lays more stress on the importance of the individual but the individual himself has a greater self-consciousness.[2] This emphasis on individuality and self-consciousness is reflected in Western religion. Here the cult of the human personality is developed to the degree that a great number of Christians accept the doctrine of the resurrection of

1 *A Theory of Disease.* George Allen and Unwin. 1957.
2 One is here using self-consciousness in the every-day sense of the word.

the body. Modernists may urge that this is no longer believed in the literal sense of the term but in so doing they are speaking for themselves rather than for the whole mass of believers. Even if we do not accept that we persist after death in corporeal form or in some shadowy equivalent of it, we are still dedicated to the idea of personal survival. We continue as our at any rate spiritual selves throughout eternity or until the day of judgement. There is nothing equivalent to this belief in Buddhism or Hinduism. For us salvation consists in being saved and in persisting as ourselves. It is constantly urged on behalf of Christianity that it gave man hope of survival. Certainly it did and from some points of view this is among the religion's chief weaknesses. The more we insist on the importance of human individuality the more we facilitate the operation of those psychiatric forces which tend to destroy it. The more the individual is aware of the clear demarcation of his personality the more insecure he feels in relation both to the herd and the forces of nature. On the other hand, the more the individual feels himself merged with the Absolute the less he is prone to neurosis. In the East the true believer endeavours to merge himself with the Absolute even in this life. In Christianity the individual is denied even this privilege in death. By his own egotistical interpretation of the doctrine of the Resurrection he still clings to the idea of the survival of personality after the death of his body. But the supreme happiness is the achievement of Oneness, in being joined to God and to all things visible and invisible. In orthodox Christianity even the saved soul is still separate. We will sit on the right hand of God in the Glory of the Father. Heaven is full of majesty and glory but there will, even in our glory, be separation from the Father, the Son and the Angels. It is easy for less rigid churchmen to say that no one claims to know the substance of Eternity and that the conception of Heaven as described above is merely of symbolic significance. But the mass of orthodox believers think in such terms and I would hazard that in this matter a great number of priests hold similar opinions. I think it quite inevitable that this should be so. Once you accept the principle of God as a personality you are well on the way to a heaven of multiple voices. When you add to it the belief in the survival of personality you are still further on the same road. At any rate the persistence of the separate personality is, to millions of orthodox Christians, something to be striven for. The idea of apartness after death increases the sense of separation and with it the sense of insecurity during life.

The orthodox Christian may react violently to this view because at the conscious level he dreads personal annihilation. But this particular dread is enhanced, if not initiated, by the doctrine of personal survival. Also the orthodox believer has no inkling of the force of the death wish within him.[3] His conscious dread of annihilation is to some extent a compensation for it.

Certainly the idea that this life in which we are imprisoned is not the whole of our existence is one of the most comforting thoughts afforded us. Where Christianity errs is that it has sought to mould the form of eternity into a dogma which can only increase the stresses to which man is subjected. In the West we are cursed by a materialistic perfectionism. This reaches its apotheosis in the United States where the cult of success approximates to the worship of mammon. Our life in Western civilization has become largely the pursuit of material rewards. Our pursuit of immortality is that of an immaterial but none the less tangible reward.

On the spiritual plane this desire to persist as an individual may be catastrophic. It may not only bedevil our ethics and drain the virtue from our substance but may also render us more prone to neurotic disturbances. The type of person who is so preoccupied with the saving of his soul that his holiness becomes indistinguishable from egoism is not uncommon. There are many who are prepared to save their souls at the expense of other people's bodies. For them life is a careful and self-conscious assessment of a system of rewards and punishments. These attempts to carry self-consciousness across the frontiers of eternity are for the most part morbid. The essence of religion, and of happiness, is self surrender. We may, as an outcome of our submission to God or the Absolute, ensure our personal survival but this should come as a by-product of our dedicated state and should never be an aim in itself. It is com-

[3] In using the expression 'death wish' I am referring to my own, and not to the Freudian, conception of this term. I am seeking to imply the tendency of the liberated self which, freed from the confines of the egocentric personality, seeks to merge with the Absolute.

mon to hear from those who call themselves religious that, if there were no such thing as survival after death, there would be no point in living virtuously. This unethical, self-seeking and therefore essentially irreligious approach to religion is encountered too often among the priesthood itself. We recognize that too great a self-conscious appreciation of our own individuality is both a sign of and a guarantee of our insecurity. Where one of the absolute fundamentals of our faith is an insistence on our own survival after death, our intense insecurity is expressing itself in a horror of annihilation. In clinging to such beliefs the individual is clinging to himself and such an acrobatic feat is the essence of morbidity. He that loseth his life shall save it and he that saveth his life shall lose it.

The degree to which a person is insecure and neurotic can be measured to a considerable extent by his dread of annihilation. The neurotic clings to the self which he has, to a large extent, found to be intolerable. This dread of annihilation, on the conscious level, is present to some degree in the majority of Christians. This is the reason why death among us is regarded with horror. But because this dread is so common we cannot regard its development as conspicuously neurotic when considered against the background of Christianity. It would of necessity be considered morbid in a community of practising Buddhists for whom death is of the nature of a release. But a fanatical insistence on personal survival is accompanied almost always by other neurotic signs in the individuals concerned. It is often merely the ultimate limit of their stupendous egocentricity.

Personal immortality is for the average Christian the supreme reward. From the spiritual point of view all seeking of rewards is suspect and probably irreligious. What we are more concerned with here is as to whether this search is neurotic. Now anything which increases the individual's consciousness of himself is morbid. In all illness, whether psychiatric or physical, and in all human misery, the individual's awareness of himself as a separate entity is increased. Any religion of prohibitions and exhortations, with its accompanying system of punishments and rewards, can only heighten our morbid self-awareness. To seek directly the salvation of our personalities is a positive aim we further on our own behalf. The desire to conserve our personality is the last egoism and the neurosis which accompanies it is a form of impiety. It is necessary to die in life in order to live eternally. To seek positively, in this life, an eternal existence is to fall into the error of the obsessional, who sets too high a value on his individuality and wrecks himself and his happiness in the process.

Wherever religions enunciate specific codes of conduct as part of what is expected of the believer it will be found that the reward of personal immortality is usually in the picture. An ethical code is not the mainspring of any religion and does not necessarily derive from it. The guiding principle of religion is a felt reality which determines the individual's actions for him and does not seek or require to confine him within an ethical system. Seek ye first the Kingdom and the rest will be added unto you. This applies to all real religious experience, no matter in what organized religion it may be confined or whether it occurs outside it. But some religions, for example Buddhism, do not offer an ethical code in the sense in which this is understood, nor to the degree to which this is practised, in the West. The Buddhist is encouraged to pursue Right Thinking and Right Action etc., but the nature of these aims is expressed far less specifically and copiously. They are also regarded not as ends in themselves but as a system of mind training which will lead ultimately to enlightenment. The primary aim of Right Thinking and Right Action is not to qualify the subject for a system of rewards and beatitudes in the future. One is required to seek perfection in the Here and Now. On the other hand the importance of the code of conduct in Judaism and Islam is paramount. In Christianity the idea that the ethical code is a vital part of the religion still persists and indeed dies hard. The Ten Commandments of Jewish Law are still exhibited in many Anglican churches. Both this latter community and the Roman Church regularly pour forth edicts on the questions of divorce and marriage. The Roman Church lays down for the guidance of its members the most minute rules covering everything from the intimacies of married life to the number of masses and penances which should be observed in different sets of circumstances. Followers of both Christianity and Islam believe in an after life in which personality survives and the nature of which, however vague it may appear to us, is much more specifically defined than the Far Eastern conception of immortality.

Now wherever the natural instincts of man struggle against an ethical code we have the basis for neurotic reactions. This is one of the corner stones of Freud's teaching and on the whole we are bound to agree with it. If the code is merely moral, based on herd sanctions and without the blessings of religion,[4] repression of our natural instincts out of respect for the conventions can either predispose to neurosis or produce actual symptoms. Where the power of the code claims to be reinforced by divine edict, the repression is more intense and the sense of guilt more catastrophic. It cannot be incidental that one encounters such ferocious guilt reactions in the extreme Left and Right Wings of Christianity in this country. In the Plymouth Brethren on the one hand we have a moral code so rigorous that even the cinema and the theatre are prohibited as sinful. Along with this goes a literal belief in the spatial and temporal dimensions of hell and in its picturesque furnishings. At the other extreme the Irish Roman Catholic, a puritan in many aspects, maintains a similar, though less extreme, attitude.

In relation to this repression of the natural instincts to meet the requirements of a code of behaviour, the Freudian and the orthodox Christian both fall into the same error. For both the repression of the instinctive urges is achieved, relatively speaking, from without. In the case of the Freudian this repression is exercised, through the Super Ego Id, by the morality of the herd, either clearly expressed as such or masquerading in the name of religion. In the case of the orthodox Christian it is exercised by God, either conceived of as a watchful and all-powerful deity or, less crudely, through the voice of conscience. (The latter expression is very often not by any means the echo within us of the voice of God but the inward reverberation of the coercive power of the herd.) What both the orthodox Christian and the Freudian do not realize is that if our religious attitude is centred round the primary fact that God is within us the nature of the struggle within us between our desires and repressive influences is radically altered. Our per-

[4] Freud would say that even religious codes were based on herd sanctions. To a considerable degree his attitude is correct in so far as we are concerned with codes of behaviour formulated within the framework of organized religion.

sonality, in the active sense of the word, is the sum total of the instincts we have inherited and the sentiments and ideas we have acquired in the course of existence. Of these attributes our instinctive urges are the strongest motivating force of our personalities. But to live according to the principle that God is within us means that we have shed the bane of our own personality and that what was previously our pride and our burden is no longer ours but an instrument lent to us for a limited span. Our desires do not necessarily die but they cease to be primary factors.

Where the personality is engined by desires which it regards as peculiarly its own it will be subject to neurotic symptoms when in conflict with an ethical code, particularly if this latter is regarded as religiously inspired. Where the reward is the long deferred but eagerly desired prize of eternal life the tension is infinitely prolonged. To this degree Christianity with its sanctions and prohibitions, with its almost concrete prize of personal survival, is especially conducive to pathological reactions.

It can be argued that in discussing Christianity I have laid too much stress on religious observance and belief and too little on religious experience. It can be argued that of course the Christian acts as though God were within him. Certainly there are Christians for whom this is the central fact of their religion. That I believe them to be few is of less importance than the fact that beyond doubt their numbers are small compared with those who in the Hindu and Buddhist religions regard themselves as inhabited by the timeless and universal spirit. And if the Christian regards the conception of God within him as more fundamental than the specific features of the Christian faith such as the belief in the divinity of Christ and the Holy Trinity, then he is not so much a Christian as a practitioner of an early basic religion which may be at the root of all religions.

We may say that, however much we grant that the seeking of rewards is irreligious, man not only needs a purpose in life but that it is inconceivable that he should be deprived of it. But too often when we talk of purpose we are referring to our own personal interpretation of it. Purpose is often merely the sword of personality. God's purpose, not our own, is the keynote to the religious life. In seeking His purpose we are surrendering our own.

In this book I have said nothing to deny the belief in immortality. In my own opinion the evidence for some form of continuing existence is far greater than that to the contrary. All I am stating is that the desire for personal immortality may be morbid and that a religion with personal immortality as one of its corner stones facilitates neurotic reactions. The belief in, as distinct from the desire for, immortality, whether personal or otherwise, is neither morbid nor unfounded.

Perhaps the disruptive effect on the human psyche of the desire for personal immortality is seen at its maximum in the case of the obsessional type. Individuals so constituted are, as we have seen, hyperconscientious, unduly meticulous and prone to ritualistic symptoms. The obsessional tendency expressed in symptoms of disease flourishes especially in the Anglo-Saxon civilizations of the Empire and the United States. Though it occurs elsewhere it is an especial curse to the conscientious Protestant in whom desire for success and a high standard of living is combined with a well-developed social, and sanitary, conscience. This malady achieves its maximum illness against the background of a religion which, in relation to Roman Catholicism, is rationalistic and scientific, and less dependent on what it might call superstition and blind faith. In Victorian and Edwardian Britain Protestantism passed through a phase which combined to an unusual degree the pursuit of both worldly success and the world to come. To own a business where the capital value increased steadily and where investments were in Consols at five per cent was not only respectable but a sign of virtue. Success in this world was regarded as a natural precursor of a sound and honourable position in the world to come, a kind of Ordinary Level success from which one proceeded to the Advanced Level achievement of admission into Heaven. Since those days the foundations of faith have been further eroded by the advancement of science. (One of the weaknesses of faith based on intellectual dogma is that it is so vulnerable to the slick but ultimately unconvincing intellectualism of science.) The successful business man no longer spends his Sunday morning in church. He is more likely to be found on the golf course, not because he likes it but because his doctor thinks it might reduce his proneness to duodenal ulceration. The thrustful obsessional crowds more into life than it will hold. Denied the completion of immortality he tries to achieve, by his personal successes, a fullness he is doomed to forego and which he yet seeks in order to compensate for the last success of immortality now denied him by his unbelief. For essentially the obsessional is a man who needs religion. His desire to achieve completion in his own life is in itself a direct response to the belief in immortality which is so essentially a feature of the Christian background against which he was nurtured but against the supersensory aspects of which he has revolted. He rejects with his head what his heart yearns for. The Roman Catholic may practise, in the hope of immortality, what Freud regarded as in itself an obsessional neurosis. The Anglo-Saxon agnostic, deprived of his hope of immortality but still yearning for it, reveals his obsessional tendencies in his ritualistic symbols and in the disciplined turmoil of his life.

The trouble with immortality regarded as a direct aim is that, of all human goals, it is the most infinitely deferred and all such goals are a strain on the psyche. If the individual embarks on a life of scholarship, of Empire building, of games playing or of religion for the sake of the thing he pursues rather than for himself as the pursuer, he is absolved to an enormous degree from the tensions which tend to disrupt his psyche and which precipitate the symptoms of neurosis. If we are to have peace the thing must be done for the sake of the thing. But where our goal is personal immortality we are pursuing an aim for our own sakes because immortality is not something to which it is given to us to make any tangible contribution. We can say it is a gift from God. It is not even this, but a part of His nature. The desire to ensure personal survival is an ambition and all ambitions and desires for success for the sake of success are potentially morbid. An ambition is a challenge thrown down by the personality to a universe it considers hostile. The more immediate and modest our ambitions the less their potential morbidity. To desire to live as oneself throughout all eternity is an infinitely deferred ambition the satisfaction of which can never be realized. For if we live on after death as separate entities it is inconceivable that we can survive as the accretion of desires, urges, ambitions and sentiments which is the form in which we drag out out lives in this world. Our personalities, as we know them here, must then remain perpetually unsatisfied.

It is granted by most people nowadays that frustration of our primary urges is a fruitful source of neurosis. I think it has been adequately demonstrated that where the individual's sexual, creative or self-assertive tendencies are denied expression, he is liable to produce psychiatric symptoms. If we allow this, then surely the craving for immortality so encouraged by orthodox Christianity is more than ever a cause of morbidity. The desire for survival of the whole personality is surely a stronger motive force than the desires associated with its component urges. It is, in addition, the apotheosis of self-assertion. This being so we must anticipate from such a desire a liberal crop of pathological symptoms. Again, we must bear in mind that many of these component urges of personality can be satisfied without too much difficulty, especially if the individual is not inhibited by too strong a moral or religious code. The social history of our times indicates that the satisfaction of the sexual urges is not a matter of great difficulty in Western civilization. The whole tendency in present-day education is to ensure that this biological urge should be as little frustrated as possible and, very often, that its satisfaction should be obtained on the biological plane. But to that minority of Christians for whom the edicts of their different churches are still law, the matter is still one of some difficulty. The unmarried Plymouth Brother, strict Baptist, or Irish Roman Catholic does not lightly embark on promiscuousness. He is therefore, on his way to the infinitely distant reward of immortality, denied those satisfactions which offer a measure of sensuous repose to the too-selfconscious Western personality. The more he interprets literally the idea of a personal God disposing of rewards and punishments and having within his gift the supreme reward of immortality, the more he loses on two counts. He submits himself to the unnatural strain of an endless battle for his own survival and, in so doing, denies himself the anodynes of the more immediate and simple satisfactions.

It would be difficult to over-emphasise the enormous influence exerted on the history of Europe by the belief in immortality. While the age of faith persisted, and while man believed more or less literally in his personal survival, Europe consisted of states with a fairly constant social structure. Kings themselves were overthrown or assassinated but a social system founded on the monarch, the Church and the nobility, though not necessarily in that order, was almost the rule in the majority of countries and throughout the centuries. The oppressed revolted but revolutions with a distinctive ideology were unknown. Throughout European history until the French Revolution our continent was wracked by war. By the eighteenth century, the Age of Reason and the era of transition from faith to materialism, these wars were dynastic in nature and of limited scope. Since the authority of the Church was first massively challenged at the end of the eighteenth century we have lived in a period characterized by revolution and the concept of the nation in arms. In the age of faith the belief that the tribulations of this life were compensated for by rewards in the next inclined the masses to docility and conferred on most European states a traditional social structure. It was left to ruthless and unscrupulous rulers and captains born after the age of faith to make of their own lives self-contained works of art in defiance of the laws of God. Nowadays every man seeks to be his own captain and, finding himself inadequate to the task, surrenders sooner or later to excitable and calculating demagogues who all too soon are revealed as raving or cunning dictators.

As George Orwell has pointed out, the age in which man ceased to believe implicitly in the doctrine of immortality was a crucial watershed in our history. It is hard to deny the truth of this contention. What an indictment of man this is and how graphically it illustrates how insecure his faith was even in those ages when it seemed all powerful. How much it suggests that much of what passed for faith was so much religiosity. A people which goes berserk when it has abandoned a religious for a secular idea has never known in its heart the meanings of religion. It has been as psychologically insecure in its religious as in its secular phase. In the former it was coerced into a vulnerable and half comprehended version of security. In its latter phase it betrayed the essential insecurity and the violent reactions of the deceived child.

III

LIMITATIONS OF THE THEOLOGICAL APPROACH

There are two essential differences between orthodox Christianity and the Far Eastern religions. The former faith rests on intellectual concepts, such as the doctrines of the Virgin Birth, the Incarnation and the Holy Trinity, which produce a spiritual harvest in a long-deferred future. The latter are more concerned with immediate states of mind and feeling induced by religious practices designed to produce more or less immediate spiritual effects.[5] Among other things, the devoté is taught to adopt certain bodily attitudes and to regulate his breathing. Very often he fasts, or adopts a special diet, but whereas fasting to the Christian is chiefly either commemorative or an act of respect, to the Hindu it is a physical technique adopted because it is conducive to the spiritual climate in which he proposes to live. In short, the Hindu is enabled at least to begin approaching God as soon as he wishes. From the outset of his devotions he acquires the means whereby he will establish contact with reality. The postures, the systems of breathing and of bodily relaxation he adopts are all designed to produce spiritual states enabling him to feel God with his whole being. His mind and his body are employed to relax each other and so to induce states of being in which he is enabled to release his imprisoned soul and thus to apprehend reality. In short, he employs his whole nature, mind, body and soul, for the immediate aim of merging with the Absolute in his own lifetime. Naturally I am using the adjective immediate in a relative sense. The spiritual practices of the Easterner must essentially be spread over years and in some cases demand the total devotion of his every minute. But essentially the Hindu or Buddhist who takes his religion seriously approaches an earlier and more total apprehension of the Infinite than the Christian. The latter seeks a

[5] Hinduism and Buddhism are sometimes described as more intellectual religions than Christianity. This is a gross fallacy. I can only think that the term intellectual is crudely applied to them because the practice of these religions involves what we may call mind control. This latter phenomenon is not, however, a purely intellectual process. It involves considerations of posture and in some of the Hindu faiths the regulation of breathing. The aim of the meditations in these religions is ultimately the emptying of the mind, so that the devoté becomes a perceiving rather than a thinking being. To refer to such religions as more intellectual than Christianity, with its complex theology, is surely erroneous.

distant salvation and searches for reality through intellectual concepts which only too often marr its nature. At the same time he is living an anachronism. Not only is his intellect inadequate to enable him to comprehend God but, in addition, his priests will tell him that it was never intended to do so. They may even urge him to throw it overboard and have faith but it is only in rare cases that they give him any useful guidance as to how to acquire this desirable asset. He is almost never instructed in those meditative practices which might enable him to do so. There is evidence in the immediate present that this state of affairs is being remedied. A number of those nurtured in Christianity are now utilizing the wisdom of the Far Eastern religions and philosophies in order to achieve contact with reality. The examples of Mr. Aldous Huxley and Mr. Isherwood are cases in point. In addition there are indications that those who still regard themselves as orthodox Christians are turning to the East in order to revivify and make more real their own faith. (As a sad corollary there is too much evidence that the East is thrusting after the materialism which is mutilating Western civilization and culture.) I wonder, however, whether in seeking to adapt the wisdom of the East to Western needs, the Christian is not in actual fact abandoning his Christianity in favour of a more basic religion underlying not only his own but also Buddhism, Hinduism and possibly Taoism.

The limited and fragmented Western approach to God has a disruptive effect on the psyche. The Eastern techniques render the total submission to the Absolute a much more immediate proposition. To merge one's personality in the Infinite in the course of earthly existence is to render it relatively exempt from the stresses which produce symptoms in those too aware of the apartness of their individualities. In virtue of the states of feeling he can induce in himself the practitioner of Hinduism or Buddhism is able to feel with conviction that he is on the right path at a much earlier date than his Christian counterpart. Even to feel oneself on the righ path is an infinite blessing. It does at least convey an inward assurance which serves as a bulwark against neurotic reactions. The Christian is too often denied this inward assurance. He may assert with conviction his certain belief in the theological dogma of his faith and may be ardent in his religious observances. But the fanaticism and bigotry of some of the Christian sects are in themselves evidence of the insecurity which underlies them. When the Inquisition persecuted heretics it did not do so because it knew it was right but because it feared it was wrong. Blessed with inward, *felt*, non-ratiocinative certainties men do not persecute. The elaborate theology of Christianity expressed what its constructors hoped for and insisted on with their minds. It revealed also the counterweight of doubt which they feared with their hearts. Every Christian who ever persecuted a fellow being because the latter did not believe in the immortality of the soul or the divinity of Christ was agreeing with his victim. In all religion based on theological concepts and embodying any promise of rewards and punishments, however refined the rewards and however escapable the punishments, we are faced with this war of the head and heart, of the conscious and the unconscious, which remains unresolved in the life of the individual and which induces all manner of morbid reactions.

The Buddhist and Hindu are in a better position to escape the state of conflict experienced by the Christian on the road to immortality. The practitioners of the Far Eastern religions are not seeking as a primary aim the reward of personal survival, but the Yogi who has advanced sufficiently on the path of enlightenment has intimations of immortality when he has learned to perceive the timeless.

IV

CHRISTIANITY AND TIME

In the religions of the Far East the Absolute is regarded as freed from considerations of time and space. The earth is not regarded as a testing ground where the acolyte serves an apprenticeship to fit him for the higher and later qualification of heaven. The universal spirit is regarded as in everything and at all times so that space and time are themselves of the nature of abstractions. Those devoted to the mystical aspects of the Eastern religions and who practice their special postural and meditative techniques are enabled to achieve a state of being in which considerations of time and space are annihilated. Such states of being have also been achieved from time to time by

Christian mystics in moments of revelation, but what our mystical poets have seen fit to celebrate in verse is a common experience to the Hindu or Buddhist devoted to the meditative aspects of his faith. It is something for which a large number of Hindus and Buddhists are prepared to train in the same way as we in the West are prepared to devote ourselves to the improvement of our tennis and golf. Yet it should not be thought that for the real religious devoté in the Far East the achievement of these states of being is the true goal. This would be altogether too positive an aim for those dedicated to the principle of self-annihilation. All that the utterly sincere practitioner of these faiths desires is to shed his egocentric personality in the Here and Now.

The Christian desire for the deferred goal of personal immortality is related to other important characteristics of the Christian faith which are endowed with the same tendency to pathological reactions. The degree to which certain considerations of time enter into Christianity is unfortunate.

Here in the West our life is bedevilled by considerations of time. So many of our neurotic and functional illnesses are associated with attempts to keep up with a too ruthless time schedule. I have said elsewhere in this book and still more fully in another that psychiatric disease is associated with an increased awareness on our own part of our separate identity as individuals. Now the individual's perception of time is not only an important factor in the development of his personality. It is also one of the chief challenges offered to it. The unnatural and obsessive drive which is producing the disintegration of Western civilization and causing so much neurosis in its members measures itself constantly against considerations of time. As the individual passes from one success to another in his pursuit of material benefit and social prestige, he does so with his eye on the clock. This is inevitable in that he is living in a community where so many of his fellows are similarly engaged and where to maintain the rhythm of success implies also the maintenance of an unnatural tempo. After all, the very word drive, which is a basic feature of the obsessional state, is an attempt to jump the pistol. From some points of view we have become almost worshippers of time, in the same sense as the followers of Zoroaster were worshippers of the sun. In the business world we are exhorted that time is money. Hospitals, homes, business houses and factories are constantly equipped and re-equipped with time-saving devices. This particular hilarious futility enables the executive, having saved time in one direction, to rush to save more in another, in order to free himself for still more activity devoid of any real as distinct from material purpose. We even find in our factories an unfortunate oppressed class of oppressors called progress chasers. These gentlemen are required to hurry the rank and file in the interests of increased output. The results achieved are charted up on complicated graphs which the progress chaser may memorize as a diversion while undergoing treatment for his duodenal ulcer or anxiety state.

This sense of hurry, this belief that destiny is catching up on us, has been with Western civilization throughout its tragic history. 'I wasted time and now doth time waste me.' Even in Shakespeare's day we were investing with a golden quality something which to some of the most profound philosophers is an abstraction and which is regarded as a factor of no importance to the spiritual development of man in those areas of the world where religion plays a more important part in the life of the people than it does with us. Our worship of time has been our ruin. Certainly our drive and our foresight have given to the Western world a premier place during the last three or four centuries. These virtues have perhaps specially aided the Anglo-Saxon and his derivatives during the last two hundred years. But what a brittle civilization it is! What we forget is that other civilizations lasted thousands of years and other states of Empire into hundreds of years. The Empire on which the sun never sets can only be said to have begun as a working proposition in 1759, the Year of Victories, or even later but already the sun has set over large areas of it. And what of the Americans, the latest, and perhaps the last inheritors of the Anglo-Saxon Protestant tradition? What of these supreme practitioners of the new stream-lined theology that time is money and the world is your oyster? Can it seriously be considered that a nation, one of the most sacred principles of which is the worship of success and where a man isn't a man till he has been to a psychoanalyst, can for long stay the course as the supreme defender of Western civilization against Marxism?

Is it not a case of two highly developed organs of materialism confronting each other? And what happens should such a community ever suffer a really total defeat? When you have turned the pursuit of success into a semi-religious cult, to what degree is one able to rise after defeat, which, against such a background, would be more than a calamity and both a sin and a betrayal?

To what degree the tyranny of time will manifest itself in the future no man can tell. The latest horror is the sanctification of speed in the education of the young. In the eleven plus examination the potentialities of culture are disregarded in favour of a system which enables the embryo human machine to qualify for secondary education on the basis of brittle and fragmentary answers offered in record time. This is an attempt to achieve culture by conditioned reflex. When one observes the infantile behaviour of rival motorists racing each other at risk of their lives to arrive first at traffic lights which will stop them both, it seems as though man were endeavouring to overtake time itself. For in the building up of personality as we know it in the West time is a primary factor. To lose oneself in the infinite, in the mystical approach to reality, is to be embedded in timelessness. To separate oneself off from the stream of life, to fabricate for oneself the sharply delineated separate personality which is to persist throughout all eternity, is to indulge in a race against time. After all, one always conceives of oneself as competing against others similarly engaged. In the building up of personality time is both handmaiden and tyrant. It is only in the process of self-annihilation that it loses its nightmare qualities.

It is the special boast of Christianity that of all religions it has the most historical justification. (It is a little doubtful whether this is true. The facts of Mahomet's career are at least as well known and verifiable as those of Christ.) Certainly, however, the historical facts relating to the origin and spread of Christianity are far better defined than is the case with Buddhism and Hinduism. But it may well be that Christianity has erred greatly in seeking to locate God in history. That God became incarnate nearly two thousand years ago may be comforting to the Christian afflicted with these historical and legalistic preoccupations with which he chooses to prove the truth of his religion at the cost of losing understanding of its nature. It does, nevertheless, limit the extent of God's sphere of operations. The gift of the Holy Spirit at Pentecost, at a fixed date after the Crucifixion, embodies a concept of religion which is completely at variance with that of a universal spirit infusing all things from a beginning which was never a beginning to an end which will never end. More significantly it differs totally from that expressed in the first chapter of that gospel which contains more than the others the real substance of Christ's teaching. 'In the beginning was the Word and the Word was with God and the Word was God.'

Is it merely coincidental that Christianity, which located God in history, is associated with a neurotic and time-worshipping civilization? Certainly other causative factors may be present. Nevertheless when we consider to what degree the obsessional tendency governs our life we are bound to reflect seriously that the working against the clock in this life in order to gain a reward, immortality, which is also expressed in temporal terms, is an important factor in inducing the neurosis in our civilization. For in the obsessional state man is forever seeking to create a self-enclosed illusion of perfection and even of permanence in what is essentially a transitory condition. With perfection as his goal he must inevitably be working against and not with time. Our Western desire for perfection is a self-conscious aim. Sometimes we are seeking only the perfection of the façade which is our social personality but where we aim at the realization of what we erroneously think our true selves we are living an ever greater state of illusion. For we pursue a still more illusive will-o'-the-wisp in seeking to perfect that portion of ourselves which is the bed-rock of our personality. Our dynamic personality, the accretion of our desires, sentiments and ambitions cannot be perfected. We can only release our true selves by aiming at its obliteration. The craving for perfection as we usually conceive of it is neither possible nor desirable. Perfection is only truly attained at that point when we have ceased to exist as ourselves and are merged with God. It is an indefinable state, independent of time and dramatically opposed to the requirements of time. It is possible that the Christian dogma of personal immortality has in itself contributed vastly to the excessive computation of self which is the curse of the obsessional condition. In the West this latter state permeates in its different forms both our religion and our irreligion.

The essentials of the Christian faith are that Christ was the Son of God incarnate in man, that He was born of a virgin in a certain village at a certain date and that through Him we may attain the privilege of everlasting life. In addition, for most Christians the doctrine of the Holy Trinity is part of the bed-rock of the Faith. Now these intellectual concepts which we call beliefs are of the greatest potential significance from the spiritual point of view. They cannot, however, be said of them-selves to furnish an inevitable passport to the spiritual life. An intending Christian, or an automatic Christian by inheritance and instruction, does not enrich himself spiritually by accept-ance of the intellectual concepts which constitute the founda-tion of his creed. To subscribe to these doctrines is, in itself, of no more spiritual significance than to sign on as a believer in the Marxian hypothesis. Still less do we inevitably feed our souls in accepting the tenets of the individual Christian sects such as the Thirty-nine Articles of the Anglican Church or the special dogma of the Roman community. No doubt in becoming Christians we will act more ethically than in becoming Marxists, but to live by ethical principles induced by theo-logical codes may have excellent results in developing the morality, and even the virtue, of the individual, but such actions do not of themselves enable us to grasp the substance of the religious life.

Too often what we call faith is merely homage to intellectual concepts. To say we accept the basic theological dogma of our religion is not to perform the act of submission which is at the basis of all religious experience. This act of submission is chiefly emotional in colouring but is essentially part of our whole nature. In performing it we certainly do not throw reason overboard. Faith should not only never be blind, it should always be seeing. A faith which is literally blind is a contradiction in terms in that it is only by faith that we shall ever encompass reality. But in seeking God we cannot employ only our ratiocinative faculties. If we do so we will only dis-cover a God who is a theological abstraction passed off as a reality by insecure bigots. Our act of submission demands the surrender of our whole nature with all its urges and desires. We give, in fact, 'ourselves, our souls and bodies.' Now while the Prayer Book makes this tremendous and essential recommendation it does not indicate by what means we will be enabled to carry it out. The intelligent Christian, like the patient undergoing psychotherapy, realizes that there is a long interval between his intellectual appreciation of a situation and his emotional reaction to it. He hopes that the appropriate emotional attitude will come either by God's grace or of itself and in its own good time. The majority of Christians are probably content with the dutiful acceptance of their theological obligations and with the observance of the ethical principles implied in their religion.

V

THEOLOGY VERSUS RELIGION

What we are saying is that Christianity is essentially a theological religion, based on factual evidence of a historical nature. So are Judaism and Islam. By comparison with these three religions Hinduism and Buddhism, in their greater freedom from dogma and in their lesser reliance on historical evidence, are relatively non-theological. We must face the fact that addiction to theology and the capacity for religious experience are not only poles apart but from many points of view inimical to each other. Now it is the boast and weakness of theological religions that theirs is the only way and that salvation can only be obtained within their confines. No allowance is made for the individual temperament and predisposition. It may seem strange and even monstrous to the Christian that one should even consider that to make such an allowance is necessary. He may argue that truth, like peace, is indivisible. So it is, but what the orthodox Christian will not allow is that the same truth may be reached by different pathways, and that the choice of these latter depend on the predilections and therefore ultimately on the nature of the individual. This reluctance to allow for the different approaches which are the choice of different temperaments is strange in a religion which claims as its founder One who said that in His Father's house there were many mansions.

I do not think we can minimise the exclusiveness of Christianity. If the Christian were not so convinced of the need to spread his message he would be less concerned with missions to other peoples. What other world religion so concerns itself with the proselytisation of others? We may delude ourselves that this is due to spiritual ardour on our part but what we offer is essentially a special message based on a particular system of intellectual concepts. We may, of course, defend ourselves by insisting that what we carry is a message of love but such an attitude is by implication an insult to other great religions. There is no reason to believe that the emphasis on compassion is any less in the pure core of Hinduism and Buddhism and the idea that these are what we are pleased to call selfish religions is due to a crude misreading of their import. Certainly Buddhist and Hindu communities have been less concerned than our own with the material welfare of the masses, but it is perhaps one of the saddest illusions of Christianity that welfare activities are part of the essential structure of the Christian faith.

Our religion is also over-concerned in warning us of the dangers of heresies. We still pray for the heathen and in a Suffolk church within the last two years the Buddhists were referred to as pagans. Naturally such warnings are not directed solely against other obviously religious systems but such philosophical approaches as pantheism are especially suspect and one of our more literary Bishops has conscientiously warned us against this error. One would not have thought there was anything particularly vicious in feeling God in nature. Such a condemnatory attitude is strange in those professing to follow Him who so constantly drew on the beauties of nature to illustrate His teaching.

No such attitude is encountered in the uncontaminated versions of the Hindu and Buddhist faiths. The intending devoté is advised to practise the measures advocated merely as a means of increasing his spiritual potentialities. Enlightenment may, or may not, come later. He is often told that it is unlikely that he may achieve any considerable measure of progress in view of his different spiritual and racial inheritance. He may even be warned that because of his Western disposition it is undesirable for him to seek reality against any other background than that of the religion in which he was nurtured.

Now the effect of this theological exclusiveness in Christianity is not merely to exclude or lose from the fold so many who might otherwise be within it. So many who remain faithful may suffer extremely and unnecessarily in so doing. The artist in search of the poetic aspect of reality may be bewildered by the arid dogma he encounters. He may sicken because of his unsatisfied yearnings and because the prescribed theology supplied is inadequate nournishment for his starving heart. I remember discussing with a Welsh psychiatrist the considerable incidence of neurosis among his fellow countrymen. He attributed this to the fact that the emotional needs of the Welsh were not satisfied by the chapel religions to which they were faithful and that they would have suffered less from the psychiatric point of view had they remained Roman Catholics.

Now it can be argued that this criticism is exaggerated and that there is room for a great diversity of temperaments in Christianity. It is incontestable that the faith has had its ascetics and its hedonists and these have adjusted happily enough within the limits of their particular creed. But the trouble with Christianity is that the adjustment between temperament and faith may hinge so much on hazard. While there is room in Christianity for both the ascetic and the individual delighting in the ordinary pleasures of earth, a great deal of his happiness and psychological health depends on what particular sect the Christian is born in. An ascetic would be happier in the Plymouth brotherhood or in the Baptist faith than in the Anglo-Catholic community. A person of high aesthetic sensibilities would adjust better to the latter faith or to the religion of Rome. To be attracted to the aesthetic and ritualistic aspects of religion and to be reared among the Plymouth Brethren must arouse a considerable degree of conflict. The Far Eastern faiths have the advantage that they allow much more specifically for these differences of temperament. The Christian, unhappy in his particular creed, may transfer to another, but such acts of conversion are usually attended by elements of crisis. The tension so produced cannot be negligible in a religion where the whole man is required to dedicate himself to a system of ideas which may only satisfy the cerebral side of his being and which may leave so much of his emotional life lagging hopelessly in the wake of the act of intellectual homage which he has performed.

The Far Eastern religions not only recognize that the approach to the Absolute must depend on the raw material of the individual and on his degree of culture but also that the degree of enlightenment attained must vary enormously with different individuals. In Christianity all souls are capable of salvation to more or less the same degree. This is a comforting doctrine but some of its applications are perhaps a little whimsical. There was a conference of Roman Catholic doctors some years back which occupied itself in deciding what degree of gross malformation of the brain qualified or disqualified the newly born infant, whose life was in jeopardy, for baptism. One of the particular questions raised was that of the anencephalic infant. Anencephaly is a condition in which the parts of the brain responsible for reasoning, judgement and self-control are to all intents and purposes absent. Such a monstrosity, if it survived, would be mindless from the point of view of existence in a community. To weigh up which of these particular errors of development justify baptism is like arguing as to how many angels can dance on the point of a pin. This is an admittedly rather extreme example of the Christian view that everything is open in every way to all. Still it cannot be denied that as a whole we do not admit of degrees of salvation. Such a view is indeed repugnant to our whole outlook. In Christianity it is all or nothing. Even the Roman Church with its doctrine of purgatory has the hope that murderers, sodomites, atheists and Protestants may one day make the grade in terms of full equality.

In the Far East recognition of the fact that the path to enlightenment must depend to a large extent on the mental potentialities and cultural attributes of the individual was carried to such a degree that in Brahminism those designed to be the spiritual leaders of the community constituted a special class outside of which they were forbidden to marry. Again, while Buddhism is essentially a psychological system involving the whole man rather than a theological structure, it nevertheless indicates that for those in whom the intellectual processes predominate enlightenment may be obtained by thought and in some cases even by scholarship.

Apart from these more quantitative considerations of the degree of culture, intellect or spiritual ardour available in the acolyte, the Far Eastern religions consider especially the predilections of the individual in advising as to what paths he will follow. Perhaps this can best be illustrated by considering the universal attribute of sex. For the Yogi or those entering the austere Buddhist monastic orders sexual activity is to be eschewed because it is a supremely earthly tie intolerable to those seeking detachment from the tyranny of their desires. Among those not wholly dedicated to the spiritual life sexual activity is discouraged or encouraged according to the degree of enlightenment pursued by the individual. But in addition to this in some forms of the Buddhist and Hindu faiths positive encouragement is given to sexual activity. This is on the principal that for some so constituted sexual activity may in itself be one of the recognized roads to enlightenment.[6] This is merely another method of saying that the individual may attain proximity to God through sensual experience, a theme insisted on for centuries by poets and artists in Western civilization but which has been rejected decisively by the Christian church for the greater part of its history.

This Far Eastern consideration for the raw material and predilections of the individual in relation to his spiritual life has no counterpart in Christianity. The Roman may argue that within the limits of his church both those of monastic and celibate inclinations and those whose lot it is to marry and multiply may find happiness and salvation. This is not by any means the same thing. At best this is merely a crude division of the faithful into Marys and Marthas and this is not enough to meet the needs of the greater diversity of human creatures. Again, whether the Christian is leading a contemplative or an active life he subscribes to the same fixed theological system which, in its exclusiveness, makes little allowance for the different varieties of spiritual food required by the many different varieties of Christian. Nor can it be said that the monastic orders in Christianity cater especially for the contemplatives. Some do, to a greater or less degree, but many of these orders are to a great extent working communities. This is also true to varying degrees in other religions with monastic

[6] Many of the Hindu gods had wives.

communities but it cannot be denied that, comparatively speaking, Christianity is guarded in its encouragement of the contemplatives. For the greater part of Christian history the closed orders have certainly not encouraged mysticism and have busied themselves on many occasions in its suppression. The Roman church has often shown itself sensitive to the charge that its closed orders are centres of this activity. There is certainly in Western religion no such positive canalization of mystical potentialities such as sends a proportion of Buddhists into monasteries for the specific purpose of leading a life of contemplation and which encourages large numbers of Hindus in the practise of meditation.

The Christian may claim that his religion provides for every type of man but it has never asserted that the key to salvation can be provided by any particular predilection or aptitude specially developed in the individual. The Benedictine may have served God by forming libraries and keeping culture alive during the Dark Ages. In a monastery nowadays this or that monk may approach God more nearly in the library than in any other of his activities. This may be admitted as a fact by his fellow Christians but even if this is so it is emphatically not the same as the Eastern claim that enlightenment may be achieved through a particular approach especially favoured by the individual.

Nor can Christianity claim that its attitude to sex as an aid or obstacle to enlightenment is analogous to that shown in the Far Eastern religions. Certainly it permits sexuality. It is inconceivable that any religion could ban sexual activity as a whole and continue to exist. Even the Doukhobors had to proceed to the extent of self-mutilation in order to make quite certain. But until modern times the Christian attitude in this matter has been markedly prohibitive. It may be argued that the antipathy of Christianity has not been directed against sexuality as such and that its only concern has been to restrain promiscuousness. But it is only recently that the idea that sexual activity is, for some, desirable in itself and not only a means to procreation, has become widely acceptable to ecclesiastical opinion. One feels, too, that the Church has only surrendered because it had to. In spite of the fact that one of the unique contributions of Christianity, as conceived of by Christ, was to raise the status of women, throughout long periods of history ecclesiastics have regarded her as potentially the instrument of evil. Half a century ago in this country it was commonly held that for a married woman to experience passion was an indication of her abandoned state.

It is accepted nowadays that for an individual to make his living at a job which does not employ his natural aptitudes or to which he is temperamentally unsuited, has at least potentially undesirable effects on his psychiatric well being. This age has seen a considerable development of vocational guidance in order to avoid this danger. If we consider that maladjustment in the professional sphere is harmful, how much the more so must we consider it a menace in the domain of religion. Certainly we do not want too much vocational guidance in spiritual matters. Perhaps one of the errors to which the priesthood are especially prone is that they intervene too much between man and his God. Certainly too often they insist on an intellectual discipline of the individual's religious urges to fit the requirements of the particular dogma it is their business to propagate. But what is required is that the individual's impulse to merge himself in something broader, higher and more universal than himself should be allowed to express itself on the lines laid down by his natural tendencies. These may be either perceptive, sensuous or reasoning. The different permutations and combinations of his emotional and intellectual resources may enable him to approach God either by prayer, good works, meditation, by entering the priesthood or through nature and the arts. It cannot be said that Christianity as we understand it fulfills these recommendations. Certainly the Christian is justified in saying that all such activities are praiseworthy and please God. Certainly if he be reasonably enlightened, he will admit that different individuals draw nearer to God through different activities. But this is not the same as the admission that the individual's special predilection should be used as the primary and all-important antenna by which he is enabled to feel God. Still more certainly it does not admit that his special predilections and aptitudes are of the essential stuff of his religious approach. To admit this would be to deny the Christian doctrine that grace is from God. So it is, but to the Christian the grace is inevitably from without, from a God conceived of as a personality and, except for a few, separated from us by space and time. The Eastern doctrine of the feeling approach for the feeling man and the thinking approach for the thinking man, is a manifestation of the grace of God working from within, in an attempt on the part of the individual to free himself from the prison of his personality by using the particular form of key provided by heredity and environment to facilitate his escape.

VI

THE TOTAL OR PARTIAL RESPONSE

The next item for consideration in investigating in what way Christianity may be conducive to neurosis arises naturally from the points discussed in the preceding pages. As an essentially theological religion Christianity does not commonly utilise the whole potentialities of man. It offers him a series of intellectual concepts. Unless he accepts a majority of these he cannot call himself a Christian. The Roman Church will not even accept such a majority. For Rome it is all or nothing. Attendance at corporate worship is also required of the Christian if he is to merit fully this flattering description. Though prayer, good works and the actual application of Christ's exhortation that we should love our neighbours as ourselves are also necessary, few would deny that attendance at church services is regarded by the priesthood as a primary obligation. When clerics, particularly those of the Anglican or Roman Churches, refer to practising Christians, in the majority of cases they mean not only those who adopt the way of Christ but who also attend church regularly and perform the prescribed rituals when they fall due. Certainly the aim of the priest is to encourage his flock along what he considers to be the way of Christ, but in the majority of cases he considers that he achieves his goal best by shepherding them back to church as a first and essential step. (This may seem an over-statement but the reader should ask himself how many ecclesiastics of his acquaintance are in the habit of advising an appreciable number of those who consult them that they would serve their spiritual interests better by staying away from Church.)

Corporate worship is not necessarily a spiritual occupation. When the erring Christian returns to church he is subjected to the pressure of the particular intellectual concepts of his sect. Their effect is reinforced in the Anglican Church by a superb liturgy and very often by exquisite architecture. Such factors certainly matter, but it is doubtful whether this sensuous enlargement of the supplicant's approach is regarded as either strictly orthodox or fundamentally spiritual by most Christians. Again, the reinforcing influences of tradition and the fact that the worship is corporate enable the individual to respond with something more than an intellectual submission. It is a little doubtful, however, to what extent these latter influences are wholly healthy. Religious experience is best left uncontaminated by the herd instinct, which tends to sectarianism, religious, that is to say, irreligious intolerance and even to persecution. That those who have already given themselves, soul, mind and body, to God, should encounter others in a similar state, no doubt enhances their spirituality. The spirit in each, being essentially universal, can pass readily from one to another. But the influence of herd emotion on those whose submission is partial, is another matter altogether. Its effect may be to facilitate a spurious assurance unlikely to stand the test of time.

The ritual of the Mass is in another category. Its value depends on what it symbolizes for the individual. As an act of commemoration it can be regarded as no more than a reinforcement of intellectual homage. In its more mystical aspects its spiritual value depends on the type of reaction it evokes in the individual. The mere belief that in partaking of the sacrament the Christian shares in the Body and Blood of Christ may be no more than false mysticism. This is because, under such circumstances, it is an act instigated by a belief and as such is the product of what is largely an intellectual concept. If, on the other hand, to receive the Sacraments enables the Christian to feel more readily the presence of God or Christ then he is undergoing a total and truly religious experience. To discuss the Sacrament more fully would be presumption. Its symbolism may unloosen all manner of unconscious forces and may thus enable the individual to respond as a whole being. I do not consider myself adequately qualified, either in learning or subjective experience, to discuss the matter further.

It is only when we come to prayer that we see the first indication, in Christian corporate worship, of a total response on the part of the individual. In the most sacred moments of the church service the Christian adopts a specific bodily attitude and approaches God on his knees. It cannot be without significance that over a huge area of the globe the believer should make his prayers to God from a fairly constant position. The Christian, and the Mohammedan, whatever other bodily attitudes and gestures they may adopt, frequently sink to their knees in prayer. In so doing they adopt a posture which symbolises in physical terms a sense of sin, a realization of the need for penitence and a reliance on God's mercy. Seeing through what ages the kneeling position has been used for prayer, it cannot be doubted that it must facilitate physiological changes which in their turn produce a psychological climate favourable to the more submissive emotions. In the Jewish religion the position for prayer is standing, sometimes with the head inclined. Occasionally they sink to their knees. We can therefore say that in the three Semitic religions the positions adopted in prayer symbolise guilt, penitence and submission to a supreme power, whether or no these emotional states are felt consciously. In Buddhism and Hinduism, founded less on guilt than on man's reaction to pain and misery, the favoured posture for prayer is some form or other of the squatting position.[7] It is reasonable to suppose that the latter attitude induces physiological changes more inclining the individual to the psychological attitude of non-attachment than to the remorse and submissiveness associated with a sense of guilt.

It is possible that some forms of Christian prayer stimulate the meditative faculties. This, however, is not likely to occur to any considerable degree. For the individual to reflect on his own sins or on the mercy of God is desirable and beneficial but it is not conducive to the self-annihilation which is the corner stone of meditation in those communities where the latter is a basic part of religion. After all, a sense of sin is a form of self-consciousness. Perhaps an exception should be made of the Quaker faith. The waiting for guidance and to be moved by the spirit is at least an attempt to merge with the Infinite. On the

[7] As a mark of respect they may prostrate themselves as a greeting to holy men or priests.

whole, however, Christian worship fails to utilize adequately the whole nature of man. Now the health of the individual and, above all, his psychological health depends to a large extent on his reacting as a whole. Health is an expression of a harmony in which soul, mind and body are acting together. This is a truth which applies in all circumstances. It is especially true in the individual's religious life. A religion which requires that its adherents subscribe to a complicated dogma and which at the same time does not instruct the individual in the mental, spiritual and physical mechanisms which enable him to achieve an act of total submission is obviously incomplete. The mind may accept and the heart reject. A conscious submission may be accompanied by an unconscious revolt. This is a difficulty for the Christian at all times. It is especially an obstacle to one of adult years who is seeking to regain his faith. So often he is in the position of wishing to believe and finding himself unable to do so. Much of the advice given him by priests is trivial and unhelpful. He is often advised to act as if he believed. This leaves his potential reaction on a largely intellectual plane. If he acts as though he believed in the prescribed dogma he is still leaving unexploited a whole world of spiritual, perceptive and physical potentialities. Or perhaps more often he is exhorted to await the grace of God but is given no instructions as to how to prepare himself for God's intervention.

Christian ecclesiastics do not adequately realize that to reduce the psychological tension of the individual is to make him more accessible to God's grace. Tension is a two-way mechanism. It makes the individual more aware of his isolated and vulnerable personality. Conversely it results from a too-great awareness of his personality on the part of the individual. Any increased self-consciousness is an obstacle to union with God. The practice of physical relaxation, either by means of one of the simple techniques employed in the West, or by Yoga, enables the individual to reduce his psychological tension. This desirable result can reduce self-consciousness to the limits of a trance-like state or even beyond it. In utilizing such techniques the individual is training himself towards those states of being achieved by so many Christian saints but which seem to elude Western man in his present state of development. It may be that the earlier saints in the Christian calendar practised techniques similar to those still employed in the East. Certainly they resorted to prayer and fasting. Possibly their prayers were of a different nature to ours and their fasting a means of approaching the presence of God rather than a merely commemorative or masochistic phenomenon. It is obvious that fasting in suitably predisposed individuals facilitates spiritual experiences. Again, in the ages which produced the great Christian saints, meditation was far more common and intensive than it is with us. But whether these earlier saints were enabled to feel the presence of God by the practice of such techniques, or whether they experienced their revelations without such an apprenticeship, the fact remains that the states of being they achieved are analogous to those regularly attained in the East by a more considerable number of individuals as a result of the physical, mental and spiritual exercises they regularly practice.

The idea that physical and mental exercises should be used in seeking the presence of God is possibly repugnant to many Christians. This is understandable when we realize that for many Christians their religion is essentially acceptance of its theological concepts plus a vague hope of the grace of God. Yet the Christian has for centuries indulged in the physical exercise of sinking to his knees when he prays. St Ignatius Loyola evolved the most impressive system of mental and spiritual exercises. In his reluctance to adopt such methods the Christian is running away from his heritage. And what is the significance of the exhortation that we should give ourselves, our souls and bodies? Does it merely imply that we should surrender our bodily appetites? Possibly, but the rejection of the flesh throughout Christian history has been too automatic to be convincing. Might not the meaning implied be simple and direct, that in the act of worship we submit our mind with its problems, our soul with its crises and our body with its tensions?

It is recognized nowadays that there is a definite relationship between the individual's posture and his psychiatric make-up. To some extent his character may be inferred from the way he stands and moves. It is, however, more accurate to say that his posture reflects his prevailing mood or emotional attitude. Many postural defects in children are a response to environmental circumstances and are a sign that the child is exposed to tension which it finds excessive. Many anxious individuals poke their heads forward as though literally looking for trouble. The melancholic is bowed and seems to be endeavouring to occupy the smallest space possible. At the present time remedial exercises are in most cases merely considered from the orthopaedic point of view. They are intended to correct the immediate fault and to prevent muscular and bony abnormalities which might later arise from it. It should be recognized that the correction of postural defects has wider effects. Improvement in the way the patient stands and walks provides him with different sensations from his joints and muscles. These alterations in kinaesthetic sensation influence favourably the mood of the patient and reduce his tension. It is to be hoped that in the future such measures now applied principally in orthopaedics will be used more widely in general medicine and in psychiatry in order to improve the feeling-tone of the individual. In view of the importance of these considerations for the health of the individual as he pursues his daily tasks and pleasures, it is all the more essential that they should if possible be utilized in the highest of his activities. The Church cannot afford to turn its back on anything able to enhance man's spiritual potentialities. It is more important for modern man that he should be rendered serene by whatever means are available than that, while in a distraught condition, he should be stuffed with dogma. The more he is rendered calm, the more, in his calm, he is able to detach himself from the prison of his personality, the more he is exposed to universal influences which bring wisdom to those who are ready for it. Christianity does not adequately prepare the ground for the sower. Though divination may appear in flashes to a chosen few, it is better to recognize that in leading people back to a religious existence, repose is the raw material of spiritual experience and that it should precede it.

We have argued that one of the weaknesses in Christianity is that it is difficult for the whole man to respond to a creed so dependent on intellectual concepts and theological dogma. We have pointed out that an additional weakness is that the Church does not sufficiently ask of the individual that he gives himself wholly. Too much is asked of his mind and when the latter surrenders he is said by some feat of theological legerdemain to have used his soul. Orthodox Christianity asks of the individual that he should have faith but it is questionable whether its nature is widely understood even in the councils of the Church. Faith is not a matter of intellectual concepts. Belief is, but religious belief and faith have nothing in common. Faith is essentially a response of the whole man. Belief is merely an attainment of his intellectual faculties used to enable him to accept certain theological dogma. Faith is not an acquisition of faculties but a shedding of them. It is not a total shedding but a surrender of them as personal attributes. Under the influence of faith one does not dispense with reason but employs it as an instrument of something higher than oneself and not as a personal guide. By one of the paradoxes which are at the base of all religious truths one becomes a whole man by ceasing to exist as a man in the earthly sense. Faith is both a process and a state. It is the means by which we achieve submission and self-abandonment and also what results when we have done so.

Our unnatural division of man into mind and body or, if we are broadminded, into mind, body and soul, militates against any clear understanding of the nature of faith. The fact that so much Western thought has been influenced by Cartesian dualism still further complicates the problem. Indeed, if we accept the principle of mind governing matter I do not see how we can ever either comprehend or feel faith. We would be for ever forcing our mind to accept certain theological concepts in the hope that when it encounters a system particularly to its liking, it will somehow be stimulated to a state of incandescence worthy of the name of faith. It is to be presumed that in such exploits the body is dragged along as an unwanted but unpleasantly adhesive partner, like a plain sister at a girl's first conquest.

But faith is not merely an attitude of mind. It would be odd if this were so. It is not in nature that so tremendous a phenomenon should be the exclusive concern of something which is no more than the eye of being. The concept of mind as the supreme governing mechanism of the individual is no longer tenable. Mind itself is influenced and moulded by too many glandular and visceral activities for it to be regarded as the supreme arbiter of our destiny. Nor can faith be regarded as the concern of the soul alone, or of some complex of soul and mind, or of any particular combination of the three artificial components of soul, mind and body. Faith is an attribute of the whole being. It is not only the concern of the social and dynamic personalities which constitute our human personality but also of our original essence persisting in us as the You which is not You.[8]

It is under the direction of the You which is not You that we receive the original impetus to faith. The soul awakening within us may stir the mind to acceptance of some particular form of religion most suited to our intellectual predilections. Such a function of the You which is not You, is, however, of secondary importance. Its main activity is to condition the mind to a state of acceptance, until the will of the individual is subjected to the Divine purpose and the personality ceases to function as an individual and becomes an instrument. The transformation of the mind from an acquisitive to a receptive mechanism is accompanied by diverse changes in the activities of the glands and of the autonomic nervous system which are both responsible for the expression of the individual's emotional life. Conversely, the activation of the You which is not You may be facilitated by changes in the physical and mental climate of the individual. The reduction of the stresses and strains of existence by a modification in the individual's pattern of life may cause a reduction in the over-activity of the autonomic and glandular systems. The greater serenity so produced may provide an opportunity for the activation of the soul within us. It is for this reason that anything which reduces our psycho-physical tension is of potential spiritual value. Repose, relaxation exercises, meditation and even drugs may all be of value in preparing us for the impact of faith. Faith possesses the whole man. Its influence is felt in every layer of his being. The particular layer it chooses for its first manifestation must vary with the individual. I feel that orthodox Christianity does not make sufficient allowance for this. It seems even a little distrustful of the ubiquitous nature of the activities of faith. Certainly it is too concerned with the idea that faith consists in the mind devoting itself to theological concepts at the instigation of the soul. Faith is not only a quest. It is itself a state of being and its influence is total in all the strata of personality.

[8] For further discussion of the You which is not You see *A Theory of Disease*. George Allen and Unwin. London 1957.

Though in this section we are considering the particular question of the triad of soul, mind and body in relation to faith, there are two other points in which the interplay of these components are important and which should be mentioned. In the sphere of psychosomatic medicine we have come to study the effect of mind and emotion on bodily function. It should be realized that the effect of mind on body would be less if these two abstractions still considered as entities were less arbitrarily divided by Christianity. We are all the victims of suggestion and of the mass mind and mass consciousness within us and it may be that psychosomatic disease may one day diminish when we abandon the concept of a directing mind governing a subservient body.

It need hardly be added that the Christian idea of the body as a separate appendage and a moral snare has been a potent source of neurosis. In this country one of the traditional medical beliefs not yet abandoned is that one can treat the mind disordered by neurosis by exhausting the body. Presumably we make ourselves healthy by punishing the hypothetically sinful member of the triad of which we are said to be made.

It is a matter of appalling difficulty for a personality moulded by Western civilization and having lost faith to reacquire it. Faith cannot be achieved by an obeisance of the self as so constituted. In terms of modern psychiatry, we are composed of two selves, that of the social personality we exhibit to the world and that of the dynamic personality which is the accretion of our urges, desires and sentiments. Our daily life is essentially a compromise between the two, with the dynamic personality as the motivating force. How can the latter, turbulent, recalcitrant and egotistical, perform the act of submission required by faith and continue to exist? Faith can only be achieved when the desires which constitute the dynamic personality are submitted to the direction of something transcending ourselves. This transcendant something exists also within us. It is repressed by the dynamic personality in the same way as the latter is subject to the social personality. Christianity does not practice or even recommend those techniques which enable the individual to free his real self, this You which is not You, and to achieve mastery of himself at different levels of consciousness. He is not enabled to accomplish a degree of self-annihilation which is compatible with faith. Where the individual claims to have faith but still exhibits to a considerable degree his former slavery to his instinctive urges, one can only assume that what peace he has achieved is spurious and insecure and a product of suggestion and self-hypnosis.

None of the so-called modernist tendencies show any signs of solving this dilemma. The modernist churchman believes that, like other things, Christianity should evolve in the light of modern knowledge. Almost always this means that it must adapt itself to recent advances in historical and scientific knowledge. But Christianity suffers from too much history already. The war between science and theology conducted in the last century and manifesting itself in such controversies as that over the Darwinian theory was essentially a civil war. It was a conflict fought between the protagonists of two forms of science both based on intellectual concepts. As the battle was waged according to the rationalistic rules of natural science the theologians came off worst. The data of their enemies was more easily varifiable and probably more founded in fact. Those who understand the nature of religious experience accept the arguments of science for what they are worth. They see in them mechanistic explanations of what is, but do not elevate them to the rank of first causes. The scientists may believe that the universe formed itself by the operation of certain scientific laws. The theologians may insist that it was moulded by the hand of God. Both are striving to arrive at truth by rational methods. Religious experience, which is the ultimate reality and truth in itself, is not to be arrived at by the ratiocinative processes of either natural science or theology, though the findings of these two approaches may ultimately confirm a truth arrived at in other ways. The patched-up peace between natural science and theology so favoured by modernist churchmen will not necessarily enable the supporters of either school to arrive at the reality of religious experience.

PART THREE

Guilt and Clericalism

I

ORIGINS OF GUILT IN CLERICALISM

From whence arises the sense of guilt in Christianity? Certainly fear and guilt are basic factors in most primitive religions but such a definition can certainly not be applied to Christianity. Buddhism, Hinduism, Taoism and Confucianism are from some points of view philosophic systems and the reflective approach to religion is necessarily less contaminated with fear and guilt than the intensely devotional. That it is true is shown by the fact that the fanatical and persecutory aspects of religion are largely absent from the Far Eastern faiths. Fanaticism is an over-reaction to fear and guilt and is essentially engendered by them. The presence or relative absence of fanaticism in the form of proselytizing zeal or persecutory tendencies is always significant in revealing to what degree fear and guilt are important causative factors. Buddhism and Hinduism are essentially attempts to escape more from human misery than from guilt. What impelled Buddha to a life of devotion was not man's load of guilt but his burden of sorrow.

All this is not to say that fear and guilt do not play a considerable part in the reactions of the majority in all religions. It is too much to expect that the Buddhist and the Hindu escape the operation of universal laws. It should also be understood that when one describes the Far Eastern religions as in part of the nature of philosophic systems one is using this term in the relative sense. Whatever their basic structure Hinduism and Buddhism at any rate are revealed as religions in the devotion they have inspired throughout the ages in millions of men of different race, class and culture and in the contagiousness of their dissemination at different periods of history.

Why should Christianity be based, to the degree it is, on a sense of guilt? What, if anything, is there in common between a beautiful faith which has enriched culture and the crudities of tribal religion? Do we exaggerate the element of guilt in Christianity? I do not think so. Suppose we reject altogether Freud's theories as to the unconscious factors which manifest themselves in religion, there is still abundant evidence on the conscious level. We have the system of confessions and penances in the Roman and in some branches of the Anglican churches. We have throughout the Anglican liturgy constant references to our sinfulness and our deserving to be punished. The Litany begins with the phrase, 'O God the Father of heaven: have mercy upon us, miserable sinners.' In the Dissenting Churches there is less insistence on the verbal ritual of guilt and penitence but the Nonconformist psychology reveals itself as riddled with guilt which expresses itself in clinical terms. It is not for nothing that we refer to individuals as being tortured by their Nonconformist conscience.

Again, the doctrine of original sin is accepted by the great majority of Christians. Is there any reasonable foundation for such an idea? Certainly there is so much evil in the world that one can be forgiven in moments of desperation for believing that we are born in a state of sin. But to do so means that we do not estimate sufficiently the corrupting influence of the evil we encounter in the course of life. It does not allow for the fact that so many of us deliberately choose to sin. Again, how can a newly-born and only primitively sentient child, be considered as steeped in sin? When one reflects on such a doctrine one realises the stunning futility to which theological theorising can descend. Whoever thought of such an idea and how was it foisted on the human race? It is a palpably man-made futility and bears all the marks of ecclesiastical manufacture. It can only be conceived of as part of a coercive system of ideas fabricated to engender a sense of guilt. One would have thought that there was at least equal evidence, considering the innocence of infancy, for a doctrine of original goodness. The latter view would, however, in spite of the considerable concrete evidence in its favour, have no value as a means of intensifying the sense of guilt experienced by those subjected to the worst forms of clerical influence. Yet the doctrine of original sin is accepted by some as a form of truth. When we examine such doctrines we see how perverting and fallacious such intellectually derived concepts can be. This is in no sense a truth of feeling such as the truth we experience when we feel God or beauty. It is a lesson to us as to the care we should exercise in distinguishing between the fallacy and danger of so-called truths and the reality of *felt* truth. Such theology is a pretentious science with myth as its raw material and human suggestibility and credulousness as its means of dissemination.

While many psychiatrists are engaged in trying to free patients from a sense of guilt, a much greater number of priests and ministers are occupied in encouraging its formation. I do not think it can be doubted that a sense of guilt and the reactions related to it are important and characteristic features of Christianity as we know it.

What are the origins of these reactions which, from the point of view of psychiatry, are so undesirable and from that of Christianity so essential and even laudable? In the first place we should recognize that the fear and guilt elements in religion are far more manifest in the Old than in the New Testament. This was because the religion of the Old Testament was at several periods of history the principal factor in maintaining the integrity and national conscience of the Jewish people. During the tribulations and captivities this people's sense of their separate nationhood was maintained by the efforts of their priests and prophets. The attitude of these latter was one which has been constantly repeated throughout history in times of national disaster. Vice, the turning away from God, the worshipping of false gods, are the factors responsible for the people's decline. We hear echoes of this throughout history from the Old Testament prophets to the age of Petain. The prophets and priests asserted that it was only by a sense of sin, by penitence and by returning to the old ways, that the wrath of God could be averted. While many of the nobler prophets must have been free from nationalist and racial motives, it cannot be denied that there is a thread of political motive running through the Old Testament. How could it be otherwise seeing that it was taught that the Jews were the chosen People of

God and that the Messiah would come, as their deliverer, to rule the nations of the earth? It was clearly understood that, quite apart from benefits in the next world, the Jews would obtain supreme power in this. This is a clear example of the fusion of religious and political motives. I think it is wrong to measure the activities of the Jewish priests and prophets against those of their modern counterparts. I doubt if they were in any sense hypocritical. Modern dictators who know the Church's coercive and stabilizing power may make concordats with it or even encourage it, as happened at the instigation of Mussolini and Napoleon, both of whom were free thinkers. But the Jewish priesthood and prophets *did* believe in the divine mission of their race and that it was designed by God to exercise dominion over other peoples. The Jews appear to have passed through phases, at different periods in Old Testament history, in which they indulged in ideas of nation worship and racial superiority of so crude a nature that they might well have slipped unnoticed into the political philosophy of the twentieth century. One wonders whether the massacre of the Jews in this century by another people devoted to racial theories is to any extent attributable, at something below the conscious level, to the fact that the former were the original propagandists of the Herrenvolk theory.

For the period of the tribulations and captivities the Jews were for the most part deprived of political leadership in the ordinary sense of the term. They were not permitted kings and ordinary political leaders by the less indulgent of their conquerors. The belief in their divine mission and the dissemination of the theory that their tribulations were due to their own sinfulness were the responsibility of their priests and prophets. The inculcation of a sense of sin was an ingenious form of mental and moral discipline imposed on them by the priesthood. Such a policy was politically adroit in that it served the ends of the priesthood without bringing the latter in conflict with the ruling powers. To induce such a sense of guilt was a partly political aim the maintenance of which became an ecclesiastical tradition. Such a policy not only served to conserve the integrity of the race as separate and apart but ensured that the priests should be the guardians of the public conscience. Coercion in the spiritual sphere has been practised in different religions at different periods throughout the ages. The ecclesiastical preoccupation with a sense of guilt is something which, if not entirely characteristic of the Jewish and Christian religions, is especially developed in them.

When we come to the Christian era we find that Christian ecclesiastics have not ceased to follow the Hebrew tradition in the emphasis they have laid on a sense of guilt. The Roman Church has ascribed to itself the right of extorting penances based on the individual's degree and sense of sin. It is reasonable that the individual should regard himself as unworthy in the eyes of God. We might almost say that this is an essential attribute of true religion and certainly few Christians would question such a view. If, however, we hold that God is everywhere and also within us, in holding ourselves as unworthy we are merely saying that the part is inferior to the whole. It is to be doubted whether remorse as we understand it and which is an inseparable concomitant of a sense of guilt is necessarily a reaction of spiritual significance. A sense, possibly a detached sense, of our own littleness and unworthiness is one thing. An intensely personal and often self-paralysing attitude towards our own sins is another. But even if we accept that a sense of sin is not only permissible in a Christian but an essential feature of his religion, it is justifiable to doubt whether a system of penances imposed by a priest can be seriously considered as a tenable application of Christ's teaching. In ordering penances and offering absolution the priest is arrogating to himself the powers of God and no argument that he does so, not as a mere mortal but as the spiritual descendant of St Peter can, or should, blind us to the fact that he is standing in God's place and taking God's name in exercising a form of spiritual coercion, however mild.

But the ecclesiastical prerogative of emphasising and maintaining the individual's sense of guilt does not necessarily achieve its maximum incidence in the Roman Church. The primary aim of many evangelical movements and missions is to reawaken the individual's sense of sin. In some of the Nonconformist churches the development of a sense of guilt is achieved not only by direct methods such as those encountered in the Roman Church but by others the effects of which are more profound. The more extreme and bigoted Protestant sects endeavour to persuade their adherents that much ordinary human pleasure is sinful. Alcohol, tobacco and sexual activity are traditional targets and in some communities not only dancing and the cinema but also the theatre and classical music are regarded as indictable. This is less so than it was a generation or two ago but this change is more due to a revolution on the part of the flock than to any change of mind and heart on the part of the shepherds. If one sees a newspaper heading to the effect that a parson or minister has been inveighing against the sinfulness of this generation, the betting is very heavily in favour of his having taken the subject of sensuous indulgence in some form or another for his theme. It is only rarely that one will find he has been excited by those sins of hardness of heart and lack of charity which should be especially deplored by the Christian. Short skirts, alcohol and promiscuousness are much more likely to be his theme. I labour this point because a sense of sin in relation to ordinary human pleasures appears to be one of the chief forms in which this reaction has manifested itself in the Protestant world in the last three centuries.

It is strange that sensuous indulgence should be such an obsession of the Christian priesthood and ministry. Certainly no such attitude can derive from the teaching of Christ. Like some other great prophets He appears to have given no specific instructions on questions of sex. In the only dramatic interlude in the Gospels in which sex is involved He intervened on behalf of the woman taken in adultery. So far as His attitude to other forms of sensuous pleasure is concerned we should remember that at the feast of Cana in Galilee He changed the water into wine. One can imagine the uproar which would be aroused and the charges of ungodliness which would be levelled at His head were He to be incarnate in this present age and were He to perform a similar miracle. Some of the leaders of the Free Churches would find this an excellent opportunity for their characteristic invective and the kind of people who respond badly to the Duke of Edinburgh's Sunday polo would find a change of target inviting. Then, too, Christ took delight in natural beauty and illustrated His parables and teachings by examples drawn from nature. This is a far cry from the distrust of aesthetic factors by the more extreme sects of Protestantism. There is not only no foundation in Christ's teaching for the Church's, and above all, the Free Churches' attitude to the simpler sensuous indulgences but the evidence of the Gospels is, if anything, towards the contrary view. One is forced to the conclusion that the clerical attitude to such forms of sensuousness is part of the desire to induce a sense of guilt. To stimulate this latter reaction in relation to those simpler appetites which are the almost universal consequence of man's instinctive equipment is to trap a great number of people responsive to clerical opinion in an enormous and continual web of guilt. That these efforts are successful is shown by the large incidence of neurosis among the more puritanical sects. It should be pointed out that under the latter description we may include a good deal of Irish Roman Catholicism which lacks the urbanity and tolerance to venial sins displayed by many Roman Catholic communities on the Continent.

We have argued that the inculcation of a sense of guilt was a measure adopted by the priests and prophets of the Old Testament to maintain the integrity of the Jewish people and to prepare them for subsequent nationhood and temporal power as the chosen representatives of God on earth. We have also indictated briefly[1] that the Christian Church, even in modern times, is similarly engaged in the dissemination of guilt feelings. Lest it should be thought that one is over-estimating the persistence of Hebraic influence in orthodox Christianity it should be pointed out that the latter carries on other examples of Jewish ecclesiastical tradition. Circumcision is obligatory to the Jew and is prescribed by the laws of his religion. But we ourselves practise this alien and mutilating rite laid down by a religion which is not ours but which still exerts an insidious influence on our own. Many of the so-called scientific arguments in favour of circumcision are laughable. It is, for instance, held to be more hygienic to be circumcised than uncircumcised. The human body, complete with foreskin, has adapted itself in the course of aeons, to the needs and stresses of its environment. It is unthinkable that nature should ensure that the human male be invariably born with a useless and unhygienic appendage. Again, our barbarous and illogical attitude

[1] The evidence that a sense of guilt is part of the basic structure of Christianity is enormous and can only be referred to very briefly in any book not devoted exclusively to the subject.

to homosexuality is carried over from Jewish law through the Canon Law of the Church to Common Law. It is significant that the attitude towards the unfortunates afflicted with homosexuality is more reasonable and humane in those Latin Catholic countries where the Judaic influence is less persistent than it is in our Protestant communities. Other examples of the persistence of the edicts of Jewish clericalism are the Sabbatarianism of some of the Protestant sects, perhaps especially the Presbyterian community, and the insistence till recently on women's heads being covered in Church. The Anglican ceremony of the churching of women is surely based on the strange compound of theology and sanitation which passes for religion in parts of the Old Testament and which erupts with special violence in the Book of Leviticus. The prayer, in the English Liturgy, for people specially designated by race, *e.g.* Turks and Jews, is surely carried over from Judaism itself. The great religions of the Far East certainly do not exhibit this racial exclusiveness, but then at no time were they ever the handmaid of nationalist aspirations to the degree manifested by Judaism. (That the spread of Buddhism was encouraged by Asoka is a different matter altogether. For a conquering emperor to renounce the sword in the hour of victory and to encourage a religion of peace and compassion is a phenomenon diametrically opposite to the religious nationalism which at different times was such a feature of the Jewish creed.) Some of these relics of Judaism which persist in our own faith are contaminated with a sense of guilt or with its induction. Others are not. But even though the connection with guilt is not obvious it is interesting to observe the inheritance in our own faith of the traditions of the coercive ecclesiastical system which preceded Christianity.[2]

To be in a position to induce a sense of guilt in a community implies that those able to do so are endowed with power in relation to those whom they are able to influence. It is significant that the power of the priesthood is on the whole stronger in Christianity than in any other of the great religions of the

[2] It is interesting that the power of the priesthood has waned in Judaism. Their present system is in no sense a clerical hierarchy as is our own. It is paradoxical that, as presumed followers of Christ, we have established the kind of clerical system against which He revolted.

world. In Islam there are no priests as we understand them and certainly no close-knit and powerful hierarchy maintained by tradition and honoured with titles. The object of veneration for the pious Hindhu is not the priest established in temporal power by tradition but the holy man who has proved his value by the sanctity of his life and whose spiritual validity rests not on the dogma he enunciates or his official position in any church but on the influence which emanates from him. The leadership of the different varieties of the Hindu faith is inevitably less coercive than our own because it is less concerned with the inculcation of dogma or with the emotional reactions, such as a sense of guilt, which may arise from it. The primary aim of this faith is to enable the individual to adopt a more spiritual attitude to the universe around him. This is achieved not by intellectual concepts organized into a system of beliefs but by the more direct method of improving the spiritual climate within the individual by special techniques designed for that purpose. With the increase in his potential spirituality the individual is much more free to choose his own path than is his Christian counterpart. The function of his teachers is not to impart instructions in the form of dogma but to suggest methods whereby he may acquire wisdom for himself and in his own way. Such an approach must inevitably be far less conducive to guilt reactions than is Christianity.

Buddhism certainly has a large priesthood but a large proportion of these are of monastic habit and not directly concerned with exerting influence on the community as a whole. Tibet provides an exception. In this country, in its days of freedom, the power of the priesthood was paramount. It is illuminating that in Tibetan Buddhism there is a considerable ritualism which would have been deplored by Buddha himself. It must also be admitted that in other areas there is a hierarchy with considerable power. Nevertheless Buddhism and Hinduism are in their purer forms essentially religions devoted to a way of life expressed in far less theological terms than those to be found in Christianity. (The earliest forms of Christianity were probably equally free from theological concepts. Our Christianity of today may be as far removed from its first sources as is Tibetan Buddhism from the teaching of Buddha.) They are to this degree more free from the coercive properties associated with systems of ideas. Confucianism, as an applied philosophy, and also Taoism, are not so subject to an ecclesiastical system capable of the widespread induction of a sense of guilt. It is probably fair to say that in none of the major religions of the world do we encounter such an organized hierarchy with so much power as that of the Roman Church. To find anything equivalent to its dominion over its adherents we must turn to some of the tribal religions.

Though it is widely accepted that Christianity has its philosophical origins in Hellenism and Judaism, there is considerable evidence that the teaching of Christ was essentially a revolt against the latter influence. This is an important point to be investigated because if Christ was hostile to the system of ecclesiastical coercion it is possible that He was also antagonistic to the idea that guilt was the essential basis on which a love of God is founded. If we consider the First Epistle of St John we are getting near to the heart of the matter. 'There is no fear in love but perfect love casteth out fear.' Fear and guilt are constantly associated with each other in the abnormal psychological mechanisms in which they play a part. The statement in St John's epistle provides the most brief, convincing and practical answer to the problem of those neurotic factors in religion which are engendered by guilt. Is it possible that in these, and other connections, we should take the words of Christ more literally than we do? The literal interpretation of the Old Testament has been utterly calamitous. Can it be that, contrariwise, we have not interpreted certain sections of the New Testament with sufficient simplicity? If we accept that Christ came to take away the sins of the world it is a little contradictory that a sense of guilt and original sin should be regarded as part of the bedrock of Christian doctrine. It is always dangerous to build theories round individual and isolated statements in the Scriptures, whether we are dealing with the New or the Old Testaments. But surely in the case of the former we are entitled to give heed to individual exhortations when they conform to the general spirit which pervades the Gospels. As the Christian message is one of love it is only reasonable to suppose that in taking away the sins of the world Christ aimed at freeing man from the torture of guilt.

The emphasis on guilt and the reaction of remorse is grossly exaggerated in Christianity. Is it not better to be a little detached from one's own sins? To emphasize their importance and to be engulfed in remorse is another baleful example of the malady of hypertrophied self-consciousness and is another form of the sin of spiritual pride. I myself find it helpful to urge those of my patients especially afflicted with a sense of guilt to learn to forgive themselves. This is something they owe to God, since without it they so often cannot shed their neurotic symptoms and escape from a condition of spiritual paralysis. And after all, if we believe in a universal God, He must inevitably exist within us and it is therefore logical and to some extent spiritually apposite that we should learn to forgive ourselves. If we are making an act of submission and aiming at the self-annihilation which is a pre-requisite of religious experience, we are not important to ourselves, even in our own sins.

To be unattached to one's own transgressions cannot encourage one to sin more. Non-attachment is a peaceable condition. It is states of tension and insecurity which lead us to err. The persistence of remorse can be conducive to sin. Remorse is a desperate state and, unless the individual be suitably curbed by an inhibiting neurosis, he may seek the desperate remedy of further transgression. Remorse is, in fact, one of the manifestations of intensely heightened self-consciousness. As such it is both morbid and conducive to further morbidity. From the spiritual point of view it is to be ranked as a sin if it be intensely developed or too long maintained.

Did Christ Himself believe that a sense of guilt was one of the prime foundations of His teaching? Certainly He called sinners to repentance. There are not many major prophets who have not done likewise. But to call sinners, a specific category of sinners, to repentance is not the same as to teach that a sense of guilt for sin is, in all humans, a pre-requisite of religious experience. Nor is it the same as the doctrine that we are all conceived and born in sin. It might be argued that in His fulminating moods Christ was seeking to arouse or activate a sense of guilt among those to whom His condemnations were directed. It is very important to consider to whom Christ's strictures were addressed. It will be found that the recipients were divisible into two categories, firstly the ecclesiastics and allied officials and secondly those who, like the inhabitants of Capernaum, had heard the Word but had not responded to it. It is hardly conceivable that Christ expected to arouse a sense of guilt in the members of these two categories whom He obviously regarded as case-hardened and impervious to His teaching. As a whole His method with sinners and the sick was to urge them to sin no more and to go in peace. This is emphatically not the same as prescribing long periods of remorse. Christ's method was essentially to lift the burden of sin and sickness as soon as possible. The ecclesiastical method was, and to a large extent still is, the prescription of a long apprenticeship of guilt and the promise of a lightening of the burden at some unspecified date in the future.

Was the teaching of Christ a complete revolt against the doctrines of Judaism, so impregnated with a sense of guilt induced by ecclesiasticism? I think it was. It can be argued that in certain passages He indicates that He has come to maintain the Law and that in others, when questioned by His enemies, He appears to give equivocal answers when encouraged to criticize established systems. But it is inconceivable that in preaching His gospel of love Christ can have supported in any way the Law as it was understood by the scribes and pharisees. It is better to admit that such passages elude our comprehension and are to be considered in their esoteric implications. Their doubtful meaning may be due to lack of understanding on the part of the evangelists, or to errors in the translation of earlier versions. Equally it is impossible to accept that in paying what seems, according to the gospels, to be lip service to the Law, He was avoiding a trap because His time was not yet come. Such methods were foreign to the divine nature of Christ. We can only regret that the full implications of His teaching were not appreciated by some of those nearest to Him.

It is hardly likely that Christianity should have spread with such rapidity had it been in any way contaminated by the legalistic and clerical attributes of Judaism. Is it conceivable that, had it retained these characteristics, it would have made such an appeal to those of non-Jewish culture and traditions? The spread of Christianity was overwhelmingly more common among the Gentiles than the Jews. To this day the Jews exist as practitioners of a religion uninfluenced by the teachings of

One who was the greatest member of their race. St Paul himself, originally a rigid Jew, was obliged to direct his evangelism to a predominant degree towards non-Jewish communities. Is is likely that Christianity would have spread among the Romans had it merely been an intensification of the faith of a despised subject people? In the first centuries of its dissemination Christianity spread as an underground movement undisciplined by ecclesiastical authority. As a religion of love for all men it was something completely novel in the world of the West and of the Near and Middle East. Its second cardinal maxim, that one should love one's neighbour as oneself, was the complete negation of the power-principle which had hitherto governed the affairs of men in both the secular and the clerical spheres. We should remember that, against the background of temporal considerations, Christ was a failure. The Messiah, reputed to come as the King of the Jews, was rejected by man and crucified as a felon. That, under such circumstances, His teachings should have ravished the hearts of men, indicates that what He taught was a complete break with accepted tradition, though it may well have harked back to more ancient doctrines which had been mutilated in the course of time by a dominating clericalism. After all, this latter metamorphosis is what occurred in Christianity itself when, after the first uncontaminated centuries, it became welded into an ecclesiastical system in which its original purity was considerably clouded.

II

CHRIST AND CLERICALISM

I think we must consider very seriously the possibility that one of the great social implications of Christ's doctrine was its opposition to ecclesiasticism. From some points of view Christ was the first great anti-clerical in the western world and in those civilizations which impinged upon it. By this description I do not infer that He was anti-clerical in the modern political sense of the term. Anti-clericalism, as we know it in modern Europe and as it has especially exhibited itself for a century and a half in France, is an unprepossessing and sometimes rather hideous development which exhibits many of the worst characteristics of what it aims to replace. It is often only a systematized agnosticism with all the attributes of clericalism and designed to coerce the unsuspecting into excesses of unbelief. Christ's opposition to clericalism was based on the fact that what it had come to teach was the rigid letter of the law, the edicts of which were regarded as in themselves divinely inspired. Christianity was a replacement of the stultifying letter by the liberating spirit.

In reading the Gospels one can only absorb their total atmosphere and adjust their more doubtful passages to the general meaning. The reverse method leads only to the irreligious conflict of religiose ideas which is the basis of sectarianism. It is very important to consider, according to the first method, certain passages of doubtful meaning. The most important of these is that which refers to the sin against the Holy Ghost. All manner of assumptions have been made as to the nature of this latter enormity. It is to be feared that the more dogmatic of these are the more fantastic. I have even heard masturbation credited with this undesirable distinction. In order to avoid perpetuating such relics of Old Testament theology it is best to make no extravagant claims in trying to discover the meaning of this doubtful but extremely important passage. One thing stands out as we try to elucidate its meaning. The sin in question is not named. It is totally contrary to the nature and doctrine of Christ that He should condemn what He has not defined. I think we can exclude from consideration any of the definite and easily comprehended sins such as are usually described in a word or two. It cannot be that any of the seven deadly sins can be the unforgivable. Why then, is the sin not defined? Is it because it is an attitude of mind rather than any single transgression such as could be described in the Ten Commandments? It is difficult to think of any other explanation. Christ is obviously referring to an essentially total tendency constantly generative of evil and excluding the individual afflicted with it from the possibility of salvation. We should not in any way deplore this lack of precision on the part of Christ. After all much of His teaching was conveyed in parables. This was not because these latter were more graphic than a series of commandments. It was not because their simplicity would commend itself to His untutored hearers. There is, after all, nothing so simple as a series of commandments expressed in terms of Thou Shalt and Thou Shalt not. Christ spoke in parables, as did Buddha and a number of Hindu prophets, because He was concerned with states of feeling and of grace rather than with ecclesiastical edicts. The nomenclature availing for the description of the higher states of being is limited and imprecise. The spirit of what He intended to convey was better rendered in a parable than by direct teaching, just as a sonnet of Keats will better convey for the majority the reality of beauty than a discourse on aesthetics.

What was the attitude of mind and heart which Christ had in view when He spoke of the sin against the Holy Ghost? It is profitable to study this in the context in which it occurs. The reference to the sin against the Holy Ghost was made by Christ after He had healed by the casting out of devils. It was alleged that He had done so because He Himself had an unclean spirit and that it was in fact a question of Satan casting out Satan. Christ said that in describing Him as having an unclean spirit His traducers had committed the sin against the Holy Ghost. Now the Holy Ghost, in its non-theological implications, can only be regarded as the spirit of love and understanding as conceived of by Christ. To be possessed by the Holy Spirit is to be inhabited by the Kingdom of God. The works of healing and the casting out of devils are performed by the Holy Spirit existing within Christ. In describing it as unclean the priesthood were committing what in Christ's eyes was more terrible than any individual sin or combination of sins. Theirs was the crime of complete lack of comprehension. (It should be noticed by way of analogy that to the Buddhist the supreme sin is ignorance.) In one of the Gospels the offence against the Holy Ghost is described as a sin and in the other a blasphemy. The latter description implies a complete denial of God and an enormity beyond the scope of ordinary transgressions. Such a description is applied by Christ not to any act of pitilessness or violence but to an attitude of mind on the part of ecclesiastics.

It is very significant that the reference to the Holy Ghost in the gospel according to St Matthew is followed by the passage in which the evil tree is conceived of as giving evil fruit, etc. It may be considered that the one passage does not logically follow on the other. It seems to me that it infallibly does so. The reference to the evil tree clearly implies that where the inner atmosphere is holy good actions will inevitably follow as a consequence. This may appear obvious but the question is why Christ should have thus spoken immediately after His reference to blasphemy against the Holy Ghost? This is surely because the blaspheming exponents of clericalism were dedicated to the principle that goodness consisted in a devotion to external observances. The clerics accepted the principle that good fruit could be produced on a sapless tree.

The question of an unforgivable sin is a considerable problem when we reflect that the whole implication of the gospels is that all sins are forgivable. If we examine the matter carefully in the light of what has been said already it will be seen that there is no real contradiction in this. Even if we conceive of a personal God, or some form of supreme being, according to the accepted principles of orthodox Christianity, we will still find that there is no lack of logic in Christ's teaching. Let us start from the premise that sins are forgiven by God. According to Christ's teaching all sins, and all permutations and combinations of sins, are therefore forgivable. But the clerical outlook which Christ deplored rendered those manifesting it inevitably liable to sin by excluding the grace of the Holy Spirit from both themselves and from those under their direction. The crime of clericalism was therefore its self-exclusion from the grace of God and its capacity to put itself beyond the possibility of forgiveness. If, on the other hand, God is conceived of as a universal spirit and not as anything approaching a personality, the idea of an unforgivable sin implies the individual's refusal of the process of self-annihilation without which he cannot merge with the infinite. As such it approximates to what in the Far Eastern religions is understood by ignorance. The individual has refused the light. All sins arise from this refusal. In Buddhism and Hinduism, even as in Christianity where God is conceived of as a more personal being, the individual in such circumstances is to be regarded as self-condemned. It should, however, be said in this latter connection that in the Far Eastern religions grace is more regarded as arising in oneself than it is with us, so that when we sin we are less inevitably our own executioners. But whether we think in terms of the

Christian or the Far Eastern religions the greatest sin is the denial of the light.

Before closing this discussion on the unforgivable sin we should mention another relatively obscure passage in the New Testament. This is that which condemns those through whom offences may come and indicates that it were better that a millstone were put about their necks and that they be cast into the sea. Offences is translated in the Revised Version as occasions for stumbling and implies the capacity to mislead. I do not think for one moment this can be regarded as meaning that it is particularly heinous to lead others into this or that particular sin. There is nothing elsewhere in Christ's teaching to suggest that persuading others to sin is a particularly horrible category of offence meriting especially dire condemnation. I can only think that the form of evil influence so vigorously condemned by Christ is again concerned with the inculcation of a total attitude. To me the passage refers to the indoctrination of others with the spirit of clericalism to the exclusion of the Holy Spirit.

Quite apart from this scrutiny of particular passages in Christ's teaching the whole spirit of the New Testament indicates that the clerical mentality as exhibited in these times was the ultimate blasphemy and the sin against the Holy Ghost. This is of fundamental importance to our study of the sense of guilt as part of the basis of Judaic and ultimately of Christian observance. Those accused of the ultimate blasphemy had been concerned throughout the centuries with the maintenance, in the hearts of the people, of a sense of guilt. They had laid on them all manner of burdens and penances the effect of which was to emphasize this reaction. It may well be that one of the worst features of this clerical attitude was its tendency to conserve in the rank and file this morbid reaction. Perhaps one of the most dramatic aspects of Christ's revolution against Judaism was that He was come to take away the sins of the world.

It is only to be expected that sooner or later the clerical attitude so deplored by Christ should reassert itself. During the first centuries of persecution the early Christians supported themselves by faith and lived securely in their own defencelessness. Having absorbed the wisdom of total self-abnegation they could be hurt no further by the martyrdoms to which they were exposed. When Christianity was tolerated, accepted and achieved the final tragedy of a need to be organized the betrayal of Christ had been completed. With the reintroduction of clerical coercion the spirit of Judaism triumphed again but with a different ritual and dogma. But however different its observances and its temporal aims, the Christian Church remained faithful to the Judaic tradition in its insistence on the fundamental importance of a sense of guilt and of original sin. The first centuries of Christianity saw a lightness of heart under persecution. When Christianity ceased to be a fellowship and became a Church it was increasingly impregnated with a sense of guilt and sourness of heart and ultimately embarked on persecution on its own account.

III

PSYCHIATRIC ORIGINS OF CLERICALISM

It is therefore no overstatement to claim that throughout the centuries the Church has either consciously or unconsciously aimed at inducing a sense of guilt in its flock. On the other hand, it would be a lamentable exaggeration to insist that in so doing it has been impelled by a conscious desire to coerce. The more worldly minded Popes were certainly capable of such an attitude but it would be a culpable misstatement to infer that such motives have influenced the majority of the priesthood. It should be understood that the authoritarian systems of ecclesiasticism are themselves to a considerable extent based on insecurity and often a compensation for it. The persecutions they have conducted throughout history are enough evidence of this. It is only those who feel themselves to be vulnerable who persecute.

Devotion to fixed systems of ideas is one of the traditional mechanisms adopted by the insecure for their own comfort. The more insecure the individual the more is the system to which he devotes himself likely to be rigid and unalterable. Neurotics who seek in organized religion a solution for their difficulties rarely embrace those creeds which permit relatively free choice of action to their members. The neurotic does not wish to be left to the turmoils of his own conscience. He wishes to lean on a system which will replace it. Psychiatrists are familiar with the tendency of those of their patients of religious inclinations to gravitate towards the Roman Church. It is not often that one finds, among neurotics, a movement towards Anglicanism or the Free Churches. Such changes in allegiance do occur. At the moment the Anglican Church claims that the number of converts it receives from Rome equals that of the members of its own community who move in the reverse direction. This may be so, but such a tendency is certainly not characteristic of those with neurotic tendencies.

Insecurity is often compensated for by naked and obvious aggression in those with strong self-assertive instincts. The enemy is struck down before he himself is able to strike. This variety of reaction is found in those who achieved power and kingship in the middle ages and at other disturbed periods in history. It is revealed also in modern dictators of paranoid tendencies. The insecurity underlying a good deal of ecclesiasticism is as a rule unaccompanied by the cruder forms of self-assertion and aggression. The insecure exponent of clericalism is not disposed to take the risks accepted by the robber barons of the Middle Ages or their twentieth century counterparts. His urge for power is accompanied by a strongly developed instinct of self-preservation. There can be no doubt that throughout the centuries clerical systems have been a refuge to those who, while fearing greatly for themselves, have been endowed also with the necessity of inspiring fear in others. The coercion they exercise is not such as to stimulate personal reprisals except in periods of turmoil like the French Revolution, when the temper of the masses runs especially high, with clericalism as one of its targets. The insecurity underlying ecclesiasticism is compensated for not only by the buttress of a system of ideas but also by the gregarious comfort of belonging to a brotherhood. The dictators and imperialist conquerors of the world have not been endowed with strong conscious impulses towards gregariousness. The mere fact that a dictator wishes at times to be surrounded by his kind is not so much to be regarded as a manifestation of the herd instinct than as evidence that he requires a symbol to comfort him in his isolation. The great dictators, rulers and conquerors of history are hostile to the herd and wish to trample upon it. Where they surround themselves with satraps they do so not because they have any conscious corporate sense but because the marshals and ministers they employ are superior slaves suitably rewarded for the oppression of lesser slaves. It is not so with those exponents of clericalism whose loyalty to the system is based on their insecurity. Here the gregarious instinct lends an added persuasion to the system of ideas and the cleric is enabled to believe more in them because others do so. In addition the sense of belonging to a community reduces still further the individual's sense of his own insecurity. These two latter mechanisms are well known as supporting buttresses for any community system. They operate in patriotic devotion to one's country and among those with positive beliefs in some particular system such as democracy or Fascism. But in any such clerical system as that which exists in Christianity, or for that matter in Judaism or Islam, the system of ideas is on the whole much more fixed than that exhibited by democracy, which evolves or deteriorates with the passage of time and where, as we know to our cost, the cardinal principles can be insidiously amended from one generation to another. (It is also significant in this connection that where the edicts of a political system are more fixed and intangible the system itself the more partakes of the characteristics of a religion, as in Nazism and Communism.)

No system of political ideas has ever maintained its form throughout the centuries with so little change and adulteration as have the systems of ideas associated with Christianity and the two other major religions arising in the Middle East. As we shall see in the ensuing sentences there have been changes in Christianity, but these have been in no sense so radical as those manifested in the political systems of Europe, particularly in the last two centuries. It may be argued that this is because the ideas they embody are true and that this being so they are changeless and of universal application. But some of the ideas which are reputed to be the fixed currency of Christianity were not embodied in the teaching of Christ. I do not think that one can discover anywhere in the Gospels irrefutable proof that Christ taught the doctrine of original sin. Many of the ideas accepted by millions of Christians were inserted into its theology centuries after the Crucifixion. (The doctrine of papal infallibility, for instance, appeared very late in the history of Christianity.) There were, after all, no Popes in the first centuries during which the faith was establishing itself. It is very significant that the doctrine of papal infallibility should have appeared so recently in the history of Christianity. This can only mean that it was expounded as a means of reinforcing the authority of the Church. It was, indeed, adopted at a time when the temporal power of the Roman Church was on the wane and when further disciplinary measures were needed to ensure the loyalty of its followers. Whatever the theological justification for the doctrine of the apostolic succession it cannot be claimed that this was contained in the Gospels as taught by Christ. The use of isolated contexts, like the description of Peter as the rock on which the Church was to be built, is well enough in its way, but even if we allow that in using the word Church Christ meant the organized and disciplined establishment which is familiar to us, it is going too far to assert that He had in mind the College of Cardinals and the numerous ramifications of the Roman hierarchy. But even those impressed by the theological arguments used to justify the doctrines of Papal infallibility and the apostolic succession must face the fact that both of these were the work of a hierarchy already in power and that the effect of these doctrines was to enhance the power of those by whom they were formulated.

This discipline and regulation of the spiritual lives of millions throughout the centuries by a system of ideas is remarkable. This is especially so when we consider that many of these ideas are, in themselves, devoid of any spiritual content and are not only man-made but very clearly serving the temporal interests of their creators. Naturally, once clericalism was established and recognized as a temporal system wielding great power and performing important and very often useful social functions, those who embraced it as a career were guided to do so by motives other than those of insecurity and self-preservation. In the age of the Borgias the Church was, in Italy, one of the most convenient short-cuts to riches and temporal power. As such it was utilized by those who combined the mentality of the robber baron with considerable vision and culture. Nor can it be argued that the Anglican priesthood of the eighteenth and nineteenth centuries were necessarily guided into their vocation by considerations of insecurity and the reactions allied to it. Certainly such a contention could not apply to the worldly, tolerant and gifted squire-parsons who held livings and maintained the *status quo* with an urbanity and absence of fanaticism which should provide a useful lesson to other sects both here and abroad. But even though many have entered the Church from other motives, ecclesiasticism has continuously called on those whose insecurity has been of the type which required a system of ideas for their reassurance and whose lack of animal ruthlessness and ardour has called for the use of threats of damnation as their offensive weapon rather than the more direct menace of physical force. Throughout its history ecclesiasticism has continued to stimulate a sense of guilt and to threaten retribution. (I do not infer that clerical propaganda has been the sole source of the guilt engendered in the minds of the faithful. I merely imply that it has exerted constant pressure to this end until a sense of guilt has become an almost automatic reaction on the part of the faithful.)

During the earlier history of the Church, in different countries and at different times, the priesthood was exempt, in the case of what was often a wide category of crimes, from punishment by the secular arm. This was one of the major issues in the controversy between Henry the Second and Thomas à Becket. Such a system must inevitably have proved attractive to those in whom strong self-preservative instincts were combined with a desire to dominate. When the Inquisition was at its height the Inquisitors used physical violence to extract confessions from those they regarded as heretics. At the same time they employed the secular arm to perform the actual executions for them. In the course of history the Church has not hesitated to employ physical force when it felt it to be safe to do so. Such physical methods have long been abandoned but coercion in the sphere of ideas is still employed. This phenomenon is still to be observed in communities like the Southern Irish where Romanism is more medieval and oppressive than in most other communities. Offences which in most modern communities are not regarded as transgressions but rather of personal preference are still defined as mortal sins and the appropriate penances exacted for them. In the more extreme Protestant sects eternal damnation is still threatened for activities which in themselves are neither anti-social nor irreverent and are part of our human nature. We should remember that so much which is condemned by the Churches was not condemned by Christ. The manufacture of sins, which is one of the basic aims of the arch-puritan, is clearly and obviously abnormal. To rid oneself of guilt by punishing others is one of the most clearly established psychiatric mechanisms. Christ preached the forgiveness of sins and deplored the tendency to judge others. In these particulars ecclesiasticism has erred greatly. It has morbidly identified itself with God, and with a condemnatory God, in contradiction to some of the most clear and unequivocal elements of all Christ's teaching. The identification of oneself with higher powers and the usurpation of their authority is one of the most disruptive symptoms of emotional immaturity. The continuance of this form of coercion at a time when the temporal power of the Churches is relatively small indicates the degree to which ecclesiasticism still aims to dominate by a system of ideas.

IV

OBSESSIONAL FACTORS IN CLERICALISM

We have indicated broadly that the clinging to a system of ideas and the desire to coerce others into their acceptance is one of the stock manifestations of human insecurity. We have also discussed a few of the associated psychiatric mechanisms. Have we any evidence of further abnormal features in the structure of clericalism?

It should be emphasized that clericalism is essentially an obsessional reaction. This might have been anticipated from consideration of the fact that organized religion is, according to Freud, an obsessional neurosis. Yet, theoretically speaking, this need not inevitably be so. Because such a community movement as organized religion betrays the symptoms of one kind of psychiatric reaction, it need not necessarily follow that its leaders are afflicted with the same abnormalities as the herd. Dictators have often displayed paranoid characteristics while those influenced by them have shown hysterical reactions in times of crisis. Nevertheless, the clerical reaction is thoroughly obsessional. It is obsessional not only at its own level and in its own preoccupations but also in its relations to God and to those under its care.

One of the main characteristics of the obsessional reaction is its preoccupation with detail at the expense of conceptions of the whole. In clericalism this is revealed in its meticulous dissection of evil into separate sins. It is revealed also in the fabrication, by a process of fission, of accepted sins into meticulously defined sub-sins. Another phenomenon of an obsessional nature is the tendency to catalogue transgressions as separate entities rather than to consider sources of evil as a whole. The obsessional believes himself to be constructive but in actual fact he wastes much of his time in destructive analysis instead of constructive synthesis. In secular spheres he may achieve much but this is often in virtue of his ferocious drive, in addition to which he frequently gravitates to those forms of employment where attention to detail is at a premium. The obsessional is rarely endowed with the capacity to synthesise. Very often boasting of his practical intelligence it is his particular illusion to believe that the whole is the sum total of its component parts. Such a misapprehension is misguided or pathetic in the world of affairs or science. In the sphere of religion it can be diabolical. This obsessional attitude was the cardinal source of the divergence between Christ and the ecclesiastics. The latter were concerned with the external categorization of sins. To them the good life consisted in abstention from these and in maintaining the complicated ritual prescribed for the treatment of the sense of guilt. For Christ good actions were the inevitable consequence of a good spirit within. They were, in fact, the natural consequence of the good man. The obsessional clerical attitude is that the good man is an accretion of good acts. It is therefore not surprising that it should provide an impassable obstacle to the teaching of Christ and in so doing should constitute the sin against the Holy Ghost. The obsessional individual exhibits more than his fellows the phenomenon of an abnormally heightened awareness of his own personality. The obsessional priest seeks to build up the human personality by a laborious piecing together of the separate bricks of the individual virtues. Yet the basis of real religious experience is the surrender of human personality and its substitution by the Holy Spirit. Holiness is not the fulfilment of personality but its evacuation.

While the mentality of clericalism is obsessed by the separate sins, in the course of its history it has shown itself to be remarkably and constantly preoccupied with one sin in particular, that of sexuality. What is especially fascinating is that it is difficult from any rational standpoint to regard sexuality as a sin at all. Certainly Christ never condemned it and His attitude is shared by the majority of the great prophets. Yet a suspicion of sex has been exhibited by the Christian Church throughout its history. The clerical argument is that the Church has no objection to sexuality as such but only insists that its operation should be limited to the confines of wedlock. This is beyond doubt socially and even ethically desirable but religion is more than a social discipline or a system of ethics. It is impossible to accept that what is intrinsically sinful should become automatically holy following a service performed in a church under the direction of fallible human beings.

The evidence for the Church's antagonistic preoccupation with sexuality is immense. One can do no more than mention a few of its main manifestations. Many of the fathers and saints of the Church appear to have regarded women as the vehicle of a supreme sin. For many of them sexual desire was a more hideous transgression than the hardness of heart and the lack of charity which are so much to be deplored by the sincere Christian. (The great sin to the Christian is the closed heart but it cannot be expected that this would be appreciated by those ecclesiastics who were themselves especially prone to this malady.) Origen preferred to be castrated and St Augustine prayed to be freed from his desires, but not too soon. One of the councils of the Church came to the satisfying conclusion that women were evil. The strict exclusion of women, even as visitors, from monasteries and of men from nunneries, is difficult to explain on any other basis than that sex is intrinsically suspect. Of course it is thoroughly reasonable that those who devote themselves wholly to God should seek to inhibit or transform what is a powerful basic instinct. But must casual contact between women and men result inevitably in the eruption of sexual desire? Such a preoccupation with sex is obsessional and, in addition, markedly irrational. It cannot be supposed that segregation of the sexes results in the suppression of sexual desire. The latter may even be enhanced by such a policy. Till recent times the monks on Mount Athos have not permitted the presence of female domestic animals within their precincts. The neurotic nature of such a dispensation does not need to be emphasized. It is difficult to think that the presence of animals added much to the temptations of the inmates.

The Church has throughout its history shown its revulsion to the human body. Its preoccupation with clothes, and especially women's clothes, has been marked and significant. The Protestant and Roman faiths have vied with each other in the attention they have given to the question of female modesty. Even in the twentieth century, when female seminudity verges on the ludicrous, the Roman Church fights a praiseworthy rearguard action in the interests of long sleeves.

The Church's preoccupation with virginity might seem at first sight natural and laudable. It is doubtful whether it is as healthy or even as religious as might first appear. The grouping together of virgins with prophets, priests and martyrs seems an undue honour for a condition provided at birth and which can even be maintained throughout life with a little determination. Certainly there is an easily comprehended and desirable symbolism in the conception of something undefiled by man. Certain absolute chastity in those appropriately constituted can release immense reserves to enrich the spiritual life of the individual. But the near-canonisation of virginity as such is morbid and hardly edifying. It is the habit of man to endow with inviolable and holy sanctions what he himself may wish to violate. Those so enamoured of virginity for its own sake have erupting within them the impulse to destroy it. Furthermore the insistence that chastity hinges on the presence or otherwise of an inconsiderable fragment of human tissue is to elevate the letter of the law, at the expense of the spirit, to an inordinate degree.

We need not refer again to the Church's disproportionate preoccupation with the lusts of the flesh, except to emphasize that this is all the more significant when we consider that this particular human frailty was scarcely touched upon by Christ,

Now in the secular world an excessively moralizing attitude towards sex is regarded as indicating an unhealthy preoccupation with it. The members of the purity leagues and watch committees are largely recruited from those for whom sex occupies too large a place in their near-conscious existence. To those for whom sin and vice, as newspaper headings, mean sexual licence, sex is, of all sins, the most attractive. It is a truism that we condemn in others those failings against which we ourselves have our hardest struggle. Whatever the weaknesses of psychoanalytical theory, I think it is now generally and rightly accepted that a sense of guilt about our own desires leads in certain types of individuals to the excessive condemnation of the same impulses in others. The most ruthless moralists are the near-sinners and many of the pillars of Puritanism are incipient Casanovas who, but for a lack of nerve and fibre, would have revealed themselves as vigorously if not competently concupiscent.

I do not think clericalism can be absolved from the charge of having, throughout the ages, exhibited an obsessive and prurient concern with sexual morality. The psychological mechanisms applying to those of the laity with similar preoccupations must also explain the same phenomenon when it occurs in clericalism. What is sauce for the goose is sauce for the gander.

We have seen previously that the sexuality repressed in ecclesiasticism because it is considered sinful manifests itself in other ways by the process of sublimation. We have already spoken of the sexual symbolism in Holy Writ and in the Liturgy and of the copious but on the whole inoffensive imagery found in the utterances of the saints and mystics. The reception of novices into religious orders is also heavily tinged with sexual allegories.

The intense and condemnatory preoccupation with sexual matters exhibited in clericalism is obsessional in nature. The obsessional state is very often based on guilt felt in relation to infantile sexual experiences. The intense impulse to atone, the undue theological meticulousness, the ferocious preoccupation with morality and the ritual of religion are the mechanisms especially employed in the ecclesiastical world to compensate for feelings of guilt.

V

HOMOSEXUALITY IN CLERICALISM

In the history of clericalism we regularly encounter evidence of repressed sexuality and also of hostility to woman as a source of evil. These two factors combined raise the question as to whether the repressed sexuality in clericalism is appreciably transformed into homosexuality. Woman is so commonly the temptress to the clerical mentality. This is not to say that the homosexuality in clericalism is commonly active and expressed physically. For the most part it is not only latent but completely unappreciated by those influenced by its subconscious influence.

At different phases in history clerical and neo-clerical orders have been accused of the practice of homosexuality. This, for instance, was one of the charges levelled at the Knights Templars. Too much should not be made of this. The use of the label of homosexuality is traditional among the human race when it wishes to indict a minority prior to persecution. It was one of the charges levelled against the Albigensians and also against the Bulgars who were among the forerunners of their faith. The Nazis spread the same calumny in order to discredit Roman Catholic influence in Germany. It must also be admitted that the Church itself has from time to time vigorously indicted this sexual anomaly. This is not difficult to understand. After all, Judaism, the origin of clericalism so far as the Western world is concerned, regarded it as one of the abominations. But the fact that clericalism itself has so vigorously condemned homosexuality is itself of significance. As I have said before, the human race is not apt to employ its most vigorous sanctions against offences which are not likely to be committed. The fact that such offences are relatively rare does not invalidate the truth of this axiom. Incest, for instance, is rare as an active phenomenon. The sentences against it are ferocious. As Freud has pointed out, such savage punishments are not likely to be inflicted unless the latent impulse towards them is more widespread than would appear at first sight. In the particular case I have quoted his researches on the Oedipus complex reveal that this tendency is far more widespread than was imagined before his day. The reader may imagine that this argument savours too much of the principle of heads I win, tails you lose and that it is too much to describe clericalism as both tainted with homosexuality and punitive towards it. But this seeming paradox is actually a matter of human experience. Men tend to condemn most ferociously in others the active expression of those tendencies which are latent in themselves. It is of significance that in this country, where homosexuality is relatively widespread and which is regarded in other countries as notoriously inverted, the sentences inflicted on homosexuals are of a blind and fruitless ferocity. The thoughtful must ponder as to whether some of the judges who issue these sentences are not themselves emotionally arrested at the sadistically homosexual level. It is also interesting that in Germany, an even more homosexual community than our own, the charge of homosexuality was used by the Nazis in order to discredit those of whom they wished to be rid. At the same time homosexuality was prevalent among the young entry of the Nazi party and one at least of its leaders was regarded as a notorious perverter of youth.

The clerical, Judaic attitude to homosexuality was carried over into the system of common law. Without going too deeply into the question as to whether homosexuality is or is not a crime, it is surely difficult to indict it as an enormous and destructive offence against one's fellows unless it is concerned with the corruption of adolescents. (This undesirable aspect of the perversion does not commonly occur among high-minded and spiritually inclined homosexuals, of whom there are many.) Yet as late as the early nineteenth century in this country the punishment for homosexuality was death and the sentence was actually carried out in some cases. It is impossible to believe that there is any rational basis for such a punishment of an offence which cannot be said to be enormously or even clearly inimical to the social system. Such ferocity can only have its basis in emotional disorder at least as profound as that accompanying the perversion against which it is directed. This form of excess harks back to the morbid Old Testament fulmination against abominations.

In concluding this abbreviated summary of the tendency towards homosexuality in clericalism two other facts should be mentioned. Firstly, it is significant that a majority of the priesthood still dresses in what to all intents and purposes are female garments when engaged in the performance of their duties. Such practices are analogous to what is encountered in certain varieties of homosexuality. It should be noted that the boys in the choir are similarly attired. This form of apparel is found principally in those churches like the Roman, Anglican and Greek Orthodox communities which are episcopalian in tendency. The cassock and the surplice are less encountered as we pass from the religions more based on episcopal authority towards nonconformity. This is of significance because in adult life male homosexuality reveals so often an excessive devotion to leaders whom it endows with great authority. The Roman Church has its Holy Father and shares with the Anglican Church a succession of father-figures provided by the Bishops in each community. The Free Churches have no such hierarchy established by tradition and endowed with a spiritual ancestry derived from St Peter and, by a leap of the imagination, from Christ Himself and ultimately from God. I have not heard it suggested that homosexuality flourishes in the Free Churches. It would be too much to say that it is prevalent in High Church circles. On the other hand, I do not think it would be unjust to suggest that its aura is frequently encountered.

Secondly, and finally, it is strange that the Tempter, the ultimate tempter, in Christian theology, is always male. Woman, generically, has been at different stages throughout the centuries the unfailing temptress to the vulnerable and watchful high priests of clericalism. But this is woman conceived of as a menace within the limits of this earthly life. She ensnares us with the concrete and palpitating reality of her flesh and leads our steps from the way of the Spirit. But the original and universal tempter, the dark and incorporeal adversary of the Holy Spirit, is always male. Perhaps in this matter theology has plunged into the deepest levels of unconsciousness and seen the shadow in which it itself moves.

In recent years there has been in this country a tendency to regard homosexuality from a more humane standpoint. Though some of the sentences are still savage, public opinion is, on the whole, more enlightened. The findings of a recent commission which studied this subject were expressed with becoming tolerance and understanding. It was significant that one of the best statements of opinion came from an authoritative Roman Catholic source. Even more interesting was the thesis put forward by a Roman Catholic writer[3] that Christian doctrine is infiltrated with the spirit, though not the physical practice of homosexuality. I have even encountered the startling and unfounded assumption that the relationship between Christ and the St John was of this nature. This, to me, is going too far, altogether too far. It is inconceivable to me that Christ's feelings for this apostle can have been described in terms of anything approximating to the earthly implications of the word love. Certainly one must reject the suggestion that their relationship can in any sense have been contaminated by an inversion.[4] We have certainly the reference in Holy Writ to the disciple whom Jesus loved. Now in the religions of the Far East the aim of those who practise them wholeheartedly is to be free from all specific human loves and to sacrifice these in the interests of universal compassion. It may be that Christianity was originally intended to give greater scope to intimate human relationships, but this is extremely doubtful. Certainly we who in these days call ourselves Christians are engrossed with, or ensnared in, such personal loves, but the orthodox Christian does not realize the extent to which his faith has been perverted from its original form. But even if we allow the desirability of these human loves, it is surely an unfounded assumption to suggest that Christ's feeling for John was of the same nature as the preference we feel for one special person among the number of our acquaintances. Surely Christ recognized that John was more liberally endowed with the Holy Spirit than the other disciples and this being so He was inevitably drawn nearer to him. This translation, in terms of homosexuality, of the deep affinity of affection which can exist between men is the basis of a number of wildly speculative and over-intuitive biographies which have been published recently. These serve to illustrate how human credulity tends to increase rather than decrease in a scientific age.

This growing tolerance for homosexuality on the part of what is still officially a Christian community is desirable as a

[3] Hugh Ross Williamson in his book *The Arrow And The Sword*.

[4] One recognizes, of course, that Mr. Ross Williamson is referring to a spiritualized and non-carnal version of homosexuality of the type defined by Plato as heavenly love.

manifestation of tolerance and humanity but it has other aspects which are not so healthy. This applies with greater force to the special plea that homosexuality is a feature of Christian psychology. This latter view is certainly not widely held but it is fascinating, in relation to what I am about to say, that it has been expressed at all. It is based on a total and disastrous error. There may be a homosexual basis to clericalism but to infer that this same factor necessarily plays a part in Christianity as originally conceived by Christ is alarming. This is to identify Christianity with the ecclesiasticism of the Christian Churches. This will not hold water for a moment. Expressed in terms of psychiatry the great revolution instigated by Christ was that He preached the pre-eminence of the female virtues associated with the maternal instinct. There are two great conflicting motives in human psychology, the Man- and the Woman-principles. (Naturally in the male the attributes of the Man-principle predominate and in the woman the attributes of the female principle.) These principles are present in varying degrees in both sexes. Many men have much of the woman in them and some women something of the man. The basic psychological equipment in the Woman-principle is provided by the maternal and self-abasing impulses. That of the Man-principle is derived from the self-assertive tendencies.

The emotions accompanying the Woman-principle are those of pity and mercy. They serve to dilute the aggressive tendencies of the male. The history of human society is the record of the different states of balance achieved between these two principles. The submissiveness of woman derived from the self-abasing instinct is essentially a submission to universal forces. This is only to be expected seeing that she is the essential transmitter of the stream of life and risks her own in giving birth to another. Such submissiveness as is associated with the Man-principle is not intrinsic in the nature of the latter. It is essentially imposed by force and is merely the dilution of male aggressive tendencies by those of self-preservation in the face of superior authority. The history of Christianity is essentially a record of the attempts on the part of a Man-principle homosexual clericalism to curb and adulterate the effects of the Woman-principle dedicted to the dissemination of the doctrine of Christian love. It is significant that in the moral issues which confront Christianity the doctrine of the woman pays should be held much more rigidly in the auhoritarian episcopalian churches with their father-figures than in the Free Churches. The question of divorce provides us with an interesting illustration. If a woman seeks to escape in divorce from a drunken and brutal husband she is afforded far more sympathctic consideration in Dissenting communities than in the Roman and Anglican faiths, in spite of the fact that the sexual morality of the former faiths is on the whole more austere than that of the episcopalian communities.

It should be remembered that we live in a man's world and that the male impulse to dominate expresses itself in clerical as well as in secular systems. The Roman and Anglican churches are far more dominated not only by the male principle but by men themselves than are the nonconformist communities. Nunneries are provided for women in the Roman communities and Anglican women are encouraged to sell church magazines, but in neither church will we encounter women endowed with the degree of independent authority afforded to them in the Free Churches.

At different periods in European history the Woman-principle has revealed itself significantly in different revolts against male-impregnated clerical absolutism. The Albigensian movement was probably the strongest of the early revolts against Roman Absolutism. (Its importance has in the past not been fully appreciated because the degree to which the Albigensians were exterminated has led to an insufficient realization of the importance of the movement.) The Albigensian faith is alone among the Christian sects, certainly of Europe, in symbolizing the Holy Spirit as feminine. It should also be remembered that the troubadours, with whom the Albigensians were closely associated, were responsible, through the vehicle of their poetry, for the introduction of the conception of romantic love into Europe. This aspect of love resulted in a cult of suffering. One suffered pain for, and through, love to a degree not acceptable to European thought and feeling in the early centuries of its culture. The aggressive and possessive love of the male for the female was diluted by a desire to suffer for her, in addition to which the joys of possession were disregarded for the more subtle and bitter-sweet joys of unsatisfied longing. In terms of psychology this involved a greater impregnation of the male lover with the Woman-principle. He ceased to assert his rights with the same force and exhibited instead a degree of submission to his lot which was essentially feminine in nature. It is of great significance that this troubadour philosophy, with its accentuation of the Woman-principle, should have been so close in its derivations to the Albigensian heresy, the anti-clerical nature of which is not to be disputed. It has been said that there was no real connection between the Albigensian and the troubadour movements, but this hypothesis no longer holds water. Anyone wishing to obtain information on this point should read de Rougemont's *Passion and Society*.

While it cannot be said that the French Revolution was primarily directed against the Church, its anti-clericalism was manifest. I have often wondered whether the habit of some of the female revolutionaries of fighting with their breasts exposed was a clear, symbolic expression of the Woman-principle. In the genesis of many revolutions against Man-principle authority the activation of the Woman-principle has been one of the main psychiatric mechanisms. It is sad that to maintain themselves in power such revolutions became increasingly impregnated with the Man-principle and ended by equalling or exceeding the tyrannies they had aimed to destroy.

VI

THE OBSESSIONAL ELEMENT IN CHRISTIANITY

It is now necessary to say a little more on the subject of the psychiatric origin of clericalism and on how it achieves its effects. As I have said, it is primarily an obsessional reaction and shows certain symptoms characteristic of the obsessional state. The most important of these are ritualism, the undue precision which manifests itself in theological dogma and discussion, and the thirst for power. How is it that the exponents of clericalism are so tainted with the obsessional tendency? This question can be dealt with under three headings. Firstly, there are personal factors in the life of the priest which make him obsessional, secondly, certain aspects of the Christian religion provide him with a special incentive towards obsessional reactions and, thirdly, the fact that clericalism is already established provides him with a ready-made sphere for the development of his tendencies.

We need not dwell too long on the factors in his personal life which tend to make him obsessional. These are such as apply in the case of lay individuals. A repressive and too shut-in upbringing, a too-early preoccupation on the part of the parents with morality as distinct from the virtue which arises out of love, an inhibitory attitude on the part of the parents towards his infantile sexual experiences, are all factors of importance in the genesis of obsessional states. In addition the insecurity of a divided home may incline the growing child to a preference for fixed systems of thought and ideas which offer to the child the promise of a handhold on the slippery and elusive surface of the universe. Some combination of these factors are common to all who develop an obsessional attitude towards life. There are no special features to be observed in the case histories of those who later devote themselves to ecclesiasticism. A tendency to neurotic disturbance may be present in the family history but there is no clear evidence that the obsessional state is itself inherited. Given a predisposition to neurotic disturbance, the environment in the child's impressionable years will determine whether the neurotic reaction to be displayed later will be obsessional or otherwise.

What are the factors in orthodox Christianity which specially predispose to obsessional states? The conception of a personal and all-powerful God the Father, all-seeing and all-knowing, and with the power to bestow rewards and punishments, is of great importance in inducing obsessional conditions. God the Father is an immensely magnified projection of the earthly Father and the impressionable child feels guilt for his transgressions in relation to Him. Were God conceived of as something less personal and powerful the sense of guilt would be infinitely less. Were the child to realize earlier that God is within Him the same relative absence of guilt would ensue. In relation to this argument it is quite useless to allege that the doctrine that God is within us is an essential feature of Christianity. So it may be but it cannot be doubted that to the average child God is a supreme person to whose scrutiny he is constantly exposed. Also, though Christ taught that the Kingdom of God is within us, the doctrine of the Christian Church very largely insists that grace is from God alone. It may be argued that this latter view does not contradict the doctrine that the Kingdom of God is within us. In actual fact it does so because the teaching of the Church implies quite clearly that grace cannot arise within us but can only issue from God alone.

The other main factor in Christian theology which specially inclines to the obsessional reaction is its extraordinary preoccupation with the sinfulness of sex. We have said enough already to indicate how this preoccupation adds to the guilt reaction which is one of the fundamental features of the obsessional state.

The third reason for the high incidence of obsessional reactions in clericalism need not detain us long. The clerical system provides the ideal *milieu* for the exercise of a particular combination of obsessional tendencies. The desire to atone, originating from the underlying sense of guilt, and tending to manifest itself in compulsive repetitive acts, is satisfied by the ritualism which is found in organized religion. The penchant for undue definition is provided by a theological system which throughout the ages has defined and re-defined the indefinable. The will to power is satisfied by the exercise of authority over a subservient flock by a system of ideas derived from the didactic tendencies previously mentioned. People with such attributes naturally gravitate towards a ready-made system which permits their expression and which also endows the individual with power in the course of so doing.

Naturally all the recruits to clericalism are not endowed with the characteristics described above. While what we might call disciplined paranoid tendencies are part of the make-up of the successful policeman it would be an obvious error to infer that all policemen are abnormally suspicious of their fellows. It would be equally erroneous to deny that many successful policemen are so disposed. An emotional development arrested at the level of sadistic homosexuality may lead some to the practice of gynaeccology but such tendencies could not account for all the recruits to that branch of the profession. Many men obviously enter the Church because it is part of a family tradition. The well-to-do non-obsessional Anglican who graced family livings may have lacked something in spiritual ardour but he set some sort of example of balanced living and on the whole was exempt from the intolerance of the religious communities to the Right and Left of him. It should be pointed out, however, that some family traditions of priesthood are not necessarily so healthy. An obsessional clerical parent is in an especially favoured position to induce guilt reactions in his offspring. The identification between the earthly and the Heavenly Father is closer in the mind of the child in a clerical family and the guilt reaction is in consequence more intense. A clerical parent may also be less likely to inculcate the doctrine of Christian love, not necessarily because he is a worse man than his fellows, but because the doctrine of grace descending from a powerful God rather than from the God within us is more likely to be attractive to him.

Some entrants to the priesthood show a modified and relatively innocuous version of the obsessional reaction. I am referring to those who, preoccupied with order, delighting in a pleasing ritual and consciously enjoying the exercise of authority (always a less vicious phenomenon than an unconscious or part-conscious thirst for power), enter the priesthood from these particular motives and also to maintain the *status quo*. Naturally such motives are only exhibited in communities where the stability of the state is dependent to a considerable degree on the authority of the Church. Some of the ecclesiastics who entered the Roman Church in France before the Revolution were of this type. Trollope's parsons were among the later examples of this species in Anglican England. With the decline of clerical authority which has occurred in practically all European countries this type is rapidly disappearing.

Certainly there are those who enter the Church for the love of God. Sometimes God is the conscious alibi for the unconscious obsessional motives. I hope it will not be considered patronising if I say that it is probable that in these days the number of genuinely religious persons entering the priesthood is growing greater every year. The fact that the temporal power of the Church is declining and that religious dogma is coming to be regarded as less important than religious experience is naturally making the Church less attractive for those of obsessional disposition and more suited to those of real religious endowment.

There has always been a leaven of good priests who, within the Church, have exemplified the wisdom of Christ against the often stultifying background of official Christianity. These men have lived according to the Woman-principle of love and pity. On the whole they have been curbed and contained by the exercise of Man-principle clerical authorisarianism. It may be merely a coincidence that the number of good men, often conspicuously gifted, whom I have encountered in the priesthood, have failed to obtain preferment.

Now the obsessional reaction has many facets and different individuals manifest varying combinations of obsessional symptoms. The reactions most present in the exponents of clericalism are the preoccupation with ritual, the impulse to undue definition even to the degree of attempting to define the indefinable, and finally the will to power. The ritualism of clericalism is characterized by a relative lack of tension. Those who repeat Litanies or pass their hands through holy water are not necessarily agitated in so doing. On the other hand the ritualism of the clean-cut obsessional neurotic is always accompanied by tension and sometimes to an extreme degree.

The combination of the will to power and the mania for over-precise theological definitions has been responsible for the sectarianism which has wracked Christianity and which inclines those of truly religious inclinations to despair of its future. No other religion has such a multitude of sects divided from each other by minute intellectual interpretations of so-called truth. In pondering this fact one should remember that the obsessional reaction is an overwhelming Western prerogative. It accompanies the march of Christianity. It is not found in anything like the same development against the background of the other world religions.

We have studied the obsessional manifestations of clericalism, the causes they share with similar reactions in the laity and the particular influence of the Christian conception of God in their genesis. It now remains to examine the effect of these characteristics of clericalism on the flock subjected to its influence.

In the clinical study of obsessional reactions we encounter a number of constantly repeated phenomena. The father endowed with an urge to power and with undue meticulousness as a compensation for his sense of guilt can, and very regularly does, exercise such domination over his offspring that they, too acquire strong guilt reactions. In clericalism we observe an analogous phenomenon. The priest may or may not have been dominated by a repressive earthly father but in his spiritual life he is subject to the dominion of the all-powerful father-figure of a God invested with arbitrary powers of judgement. He, the dominated, becomes the dominator. What is the effect on the flock committed to his charge? This must vary according to individual, racial and cultural differences and must manifest itself in different ways and at different epochs. Certainly the general tendency is to inculcate a sense of guilt, in addition to which the instruction given to the faithful is such as to augment this reaction at the conscious level. Is there any special characteristic of the way in which the sense of guilt is manifested in congregations subject to clericalism? Generally speaking, the sense of guilt is more conscious in the flock than in the shepherd. Within the orbit of clericalism it has already to a large extent been compensated for by the exercise of power and by the protective mechanism of an inviolable system of ideas. The priest feels, on the whole, a greater security. The impulse to atone is not so strongly developed as in his flock.[5] The impulse to atone, exhibited by the laity, is encouraged by penances, confessions and the repetition of self-accusing litanies. These mechanisms are not only presided over by the priesthood but in actual fact were invented by them. The power to dispense atonement for a sense of guilt serves to convince the laity of the constant and inescapable fact of its presence. The priest is therefore placed in the dominating position of a father figure dispensing punishment or mercy according to the needs of the situation. Psychologically speaking he stands in the place of God. Two or three centuries ago his power to dominate was greater than it is now and his capacity to bestow or deny absolution invested his office with awe and even terror. His power to inculcate a sense of guilt was infinite. Though less in these days it is still considerable and his office is invested with an aura of fear in the less sophisticated Roman com-

[5] The impulse to atone may, of course, be very strong in those passing through periods of crises before entering the priesthood or during their early years in it.

munities.

At first sight it is difficult to understand the rage of the Puritans against such practices as the confessional and the performance of penances. Confronted with such reactions, the tolerant, whatever their faith, are inclined to think that the Romish practices were infinitely to be preferred to the Protestant frenzies. This is particularly so when we consider that the confessional, the penances and the granting of absolution can be of enormous psychological benefit to those partaking of them. After all, doctors in general and psychiatrists in particular very often, whether they know it or not, function as father-figures and may indeed achieve some of their best results in so doing. If the doctors and the psychiatrists are permitted the additional armoury of drugs and special techniques, it is only reasonable that equivalent aids in the relief of suffering should be permitted to the priesthood. We can only understand the puritanical frenzy against such Catholic practices by thinking in terms of the sense of guilt and the clerical mechanisms of atonement. When the authority of clericalism is in any way sapped a bitter resentment is felt against the father-figure who has exacted such a tribute of guilt and whose mechanisms of atonement have been discredited. The Protestant may insist self-righteously that his objection to penances and confessionals is because it is iniquitous for any man, even if he be a priest, to act on God's behalf and to usurp His functions. This is a tenable enough argument but it sounds dangerously like a conscious alibi for unconscious conflicts. The intemperance and often hatred shown towards these Catholic practices has its origins in fear and the half-memory of past subservience.

But perhaps the most dramatic psychological cleavage between the priesthood and the laity concerns the Mass. This enormous symbol is for many the absolute heart and centre of Christianity. Now the Mass is not a mechanism of atonement for an obsessional sense of guilt. It is in part commemorative but its greatest significance is that it bestows the gift of Grace. He who partakes of it receives of the Body and Blood of Christ. It is, in fact, a reward. It is at this stage that we begin to approach the heart of the matter.

In earlier history the Mass was the prerogative of the priests to a degree not usually realized today. The degree to which the laity partook of the Mass was relatively rare, though they were allowed to be more frequently present at its celebration. The rood screen was a demarcating line behind which the congregation were excluded while Mass was celebrated by the priests. This implied that the gift of grace was to a considerable extent the prerogative of a particular section of the community. This exclusiveness is continued today and is expressed in the power of the Church to refuse Communion to those whom it considers unfit to receive it. Such a right is exercised by the Anglican Church towards divorced persons. This would be reasonable enough if this meant only that these hypothetical sinners had transgressed the law of the Church and therefore could not complain if they did not receive its benefits. But for the most part it is clearly implied that they have transgressed the laws of God. This is an unduly dogmatic attitude in that these latter laws are so obviously man-made. In addition one would have thought that the sinner above all needed the strength to be acquired from grace. As for excluding those who have not been confirmed, this is another example of the pathetic illusion that religion can be taught by a study of the intellectual concepts on which any particular creed is based.

In the Catholic Churches participation at Mass is the highest reward which the Church, as apart from the Holy Spirit, has to offer. This could hardly be otherwise in that it is claimed that through the Sacraments the individual receives the gift of Grace. The fact that the celebration of the Mass is only permitted to ordained priests and that these have the right to withhold it not only increases the power of clericalism to dominate but enables it all the more to brand with a deeper sense of guilt those deprived of the comfort of these rites. It is significant that it is only in the comparatively recent history of the Roman Church that the laity have been expected to partake of the Mass so frequently. The sharing of the gift of Grace with the multitude has coincided with the growth of democracy and the diminution of clerical authority.

It should be understood that the motives of clericalism in restricting the Mass were probably always to a considerable degree unconscious. This applies still more today. In addition their motives for so doing were not entirely concerned with the conservation of power and the induction of guilt by the withholding of rewards and by exclusion from a holy fellowship. It is not all who can appreciate the full symbolism of the Mass. Whether we like it or not it has never been the custom of those versed in the holy mysteries of any religion to believe that these can be disseminated widely by doctrine and propaganda. In this they are right, because the mystical elements of religion cannot be defined in the technical terms of theology or indeed, in any terms at all. If there is one thing of which we can be certain it is that the Kingdom of Heaven is not to be achieved by a share-out conducted according to the principles of modern democracy.

In discussing clericalism I have confined myself largely to its manifestations in Christianity because this is our particular background and also because Christianity has in the course of its history demonstrated the power of clericalism to so marked a degree. I have also considered chiefly its manifestations in the Anglican and Roman faiths for the simple reason that in Western Europe these two communities bear its imprint overwhelmingly more than their rivals. In the Free Churches, where clerical absolutism as understood in the Roman Church is unknown, the obessional tendency does not manifest itself so much in religious observance. Unabsorbed by this latter safety valve, it reveals itself more directly in the different forms of obsessional neurosis which are easily recognisable by clinical observation. The sense of guilt accentuated by Christian doctrine has not, in the Free Churches, the anodynes provided for it by the ritualism, penances and confessionals employed by the Roman and Anglican communities. The curve of overt obsessional reactions follows faithfully that of the incidence of evangelical communities and is thus found in its most intense concentration in the Anglo-Saxon Protestant civilization and its derivatives. I have mentioned this elsewhere in this book and dealt with it more fully in another.[6] It cannot be laboured further here.

[6] *A Theory of Disease*. Allen and Unwin. 1957.

VII

THE NEW FAITH

Our age has witnessed the enunciation of different systems of ideas elevated to the level of doctrine and endowed with religious fervour. Some of these systems arise to a considerable degree as a result of the decline in the power of orthodox Christianity. One cannot, for example, understand Nazism unless one sees it as a depraved religion. But leaving aside the religio-political fanaticism which has bedevilled our age there is one such system of ideas which should be of special interest to us. We are considering in this book to what degree religion and psycho-analytical theory are opposed to each other. There can be no doubt that thirty years ago the vast majority of those familiar with the teachings of Freud would have said that the two were inevitably and eternally in opposition. We are not quite so sure today. But one fascinating point will be obvious to anyone who has studied with any care the history of psychoanalysis. This latter doctrine itself bears the hallmark of religion. It shares with clericalism the obsessional tendency to undue definition. It goes to the same limit of seeking to define what is in the present state of our knowledge indefinable. It is, after all, not entirely reasonable to postulate the existence of what we call the unconscious, following which we proceed to dogmatize as to its contents.[7] We have, too, the intense sectarianism which arises from obsessional, closed systems of ideas claimed, by their exponents, to contain the exclusive prescription for salvation. No sooner had Freud achieved a measure of recognition than the schism began and it was impossible for the disciples of Adler and Jung to collaborate with those who remained faithful to the master. Perhaps it is the fate of all new religions to become fragmented when they are first infiltrated by obsessionals with a craze for meticulousness and all-inclusive systems. Certainly religions are malformed when they are organized and while organization is not always obsessional, an excessive urge to organize almost invariably is.

Again, the whole basis of psychoanalysis is the phenomenon of transference. This implies that treatment cannot be success-

[7] Freud wisely limited himself to general trends and made brilliant discoveries. Others are not so careful.

ful unless the patient goes through a phase in which he or she regards the analyst as an authoritative father. Many patients go through a period in which the analyst is half-deified. Freud did not set out to be the God of modern materialistic philosophy. His followers have nevertheless served in large numbers as substitute bishops and priests.

It may be argued that psychoanalysis has no analogies with religion because the patient is not indoctrinated with any particular system of theology. Certainly the rigid Freudian regards it as heresy to influence the patient in the direction of any system of beliefs or in favour of any special course of action. But when he offers himself for treatment and accepts the interpretations offered in its course by the analyst, he is submitting to a closed and remarkably exclusive theological system which insists that the origin of rational human behaviour lies in the resolution of emotional conflicts generated in the life of the individual concerned. He is, in fact, exposed to the practice of a theology which largely denies the existence of spiritual influences which it regards as of the nature of myths and illusions.[8] Treatment as conceived of by Freudians aims at self-knowledge and to that extent shares the same goal as that pursued by the mystics and contemplatives, particularly those influenced by the Far Eastern religions and philosophies. But whereas in those seeking the realities of religion self-knowledge aims at the realization and liberation of a self which is not personal to the individual but part of a universal consciousness, the goal in Freudian analysis is a degree of insight which permits a smooth compromise between what the instinctive self desires and what is permitted to it. The refusal on the part of the analyst to intervene when the patient is passing through crises of doubt is a negative imposition of the theology of nihilism. This two-way action of the analyst in washing his hands of the patient at the same time as he is actually in full control of him to a degree exceeding that of the priest over the penitent, serves only to accentuate his power. The analyst offers no such atonement as the priest and the patient has less security than the sinner. The latter has absolution, the blessing of God,

[8] I am here referring to the Freudian system and its more materialistic derivatives. What I am saying here could not in any sense apply to the theories of Jung.

the consolations of religion, the support of a system and the personal support of the priest. The patient has only emptiness, and the analyst. Under these circumstances it is not surprising that the latter office is so often filled by those endowed with a will to power. It may be comforting to the public to think of the psychiatrist as a dispassionate figure, caring, like Gallio, for none of these things, but those familiar with the breed will know that he is often engaged in the treatment of patients in the hope that he will ensure his own cure. Again, in dealing with the unconscious, one is able to assume with some ease and without undue risk, the mantle of papal infallibility. The unconscious is at least as unknown to the masses as the Kingdom of Heaven. Not all psychiatrists, or even a majority, exult in the power invested in them by the process of transference. The latter is, after all, always a responsibility and very often an excruciating bore. But an appreciable number of the leaders of psychoanalytical opinion are eager to sermonize or even to pontificate. Under their direction and with the co-operation of popular journalism the new faith has been disseminated with encouraging rapidity.

With its customary acuity the Roman Church has come to recognize both the menace and the usefulness of its new rival. At first entirely inimical to psychoanalysis it has now given it a guarded approval. At the same time it has taken the precaution to train its own priests in the necessary technique. (To what extent they will adhere to the principle laid down by Freud that it is unforgivable to influence the patient's beliefs is a matter for conjecture.) The task has been entrusted especially to the Dominicans. Throughout history this intelligent and progressive order has been concerned with the extraction of potential good from what has been otherwise condemned. (The Dominicans, in a corrupt age, were the first to practice the austerity and purity of living which had made the previously extirpated Albigensian faith so attractive to those repelled by the license and corruption of the Church.) It is interesting that a concordat should be established between the exponents of immemorial clericalism and the practitioners of new doctrine. Birds of a feather flock together. The analogies I have drawn between clericalism and the more rigid psychoanalytic systems should not be dismissed as unfounded. We have seen elsewhere similarities of outlook in orthodox Christianity and psychoanalytic theory, even though these two doctrines would seem on superficial examination to be diametrically opposed. It will be remembered that, generally speaking, both have maintained to a greater or lesser degree a similar attitude towards revealed religion. Should the alliance between the Church and psychiatry expand further, the possibilities are immense. It should not be assumed that such a development necessarily carries with it great spiritual gains.

VIII

GOD AND POWER

As I have said before, the sense of guilt in Christianity would be less were God not conceived of in personal terms as a supreme being endowed with limitless power. If we could think of ourselves as part of God and conceive of Him as drawing sustenance from our devotion we could be spared the consequences which follow our regarding Him as a father-figure. Where God is conceived of as not endowed with supreme authority we are reduced, or elevated to, a view of the universe where the pattern at any given time is determined by the relative strength of the forces of good and evil. Such a conception of the universe is perhaps a little more in accordance with the facts. In the light of those recent tyrannies which have ordered mass slaughters it is a little difficult for many to accept the view that God is at one and the same time all-powerful and all merciful. The argument that such horrors are sent to try us is so primitive that it scarcely needs to be refuted. This could well be the attitude of a God but not of a good God. It is especially disgusting when we in this island use it in reference to the slaughter of others less fortunate than ourselves. To comfort one's soul at the expense of other people's bodies is an unedifying occupation. The argument that God gave man free will and the latter must accept the consequences is equally trivial. It endows God with a lower standard of virtue than that achieved by the majority of earthly fathers. How many fathers would see their sons tortured, whether or no their predicament were due to their own misdeeds, and turn aside with the plea that they had given their children the advantages of a good upbringing and that now they must stand on their own feet? One of the defects of clericalism is that it cannot see that many good men are turned away from Christianity not because of its supernatural content, which some find barely credible but are prepared to accept, but because of the injustices implied in so many of its basic doctrines. In considering such matters as these the powerful Father-figure concept is doubly disastrous. Firstly, without it, there would be no guilt and no potential resentment ready to erupt should the authority of the Father-figure be undermined. Secondly, given the impulse to revolt, from whatever cause, the resentment of the Father-figure is intense and bitter and leads, if it be suppressed, to emotional conflict and, on the conscious level, to the neurotic intemperance so often associated with atheism and anti-clericalism.

It is a matter for consideration as to what extent the worship of God is truly religious, when by worship one means the performance of an act of homage to something mightier than oneself. It can be argued that the worship of God is a lot more than this. So it is. This aspect of worship I am considering is only one of many and, in my view, a deleterious one at that, but it cannot be denied that it enters into the religious observance of millions and is to many the essential fabric of obeisance to the divine. Submission is the essence of religion, but submission to a universal spirit is one thing and homage to a more circumscribed and personalized divine authority is emphatically another. I wonder, in fact, whether one should worship God or live with Him. To live with God is, of course, to accept the fundamental reality that the Kingdom of God is within you. This, of course, was the basis of Christ's teaching but one cannot agree that it is generally accepted in Christianity as we know it. Certainly it is regarded by orthodox opinion as one of the manifestations of the spirit of God but for the average Christian God still remains a distant and powerful figure Whom one will only approach somewhere in the course of eternity after a long apprenticeship of suffering and achievment here on earth. The question is a matter of degree. It is certainly possible that much that passes as sincere worship is propitiatory and guilt-engendered and tinged with a neurosis we would well be rid of.

Similarly it is to be wondered whether much of our praying for forgiveness is not, in the last analysis, neurotic, unethical and illusory. We pray, on behalf of our isolated and self-conscious selves, for freedom from our burden, to an outside authority, conceived of as a supreme Being and therefore as some equivalent of a personality. The more positive the demands of the prayer the more one is obliged to be suspicious of its nature because requests of this nature savour of personality calling to personality.

These aspects of Christianity which are neurotic in nature and, from the ethical point of view, questionable, depend on the conception of God as a separate entity endowed with power. Without such a conception these particular neurotic attributes would be absent from the religion. We cannot know, with the rational side of our nature, whether such an idea of God was in the mind of Christ when He taught His doctrine. One can only feel, with what shred of religion is present in one's composition, that such a conception of God was completely at variance with the whole tone of His teaching.

Those addicted to, or influenced by, clericalism will be inclined to ask what is left of Christianity if we expunge from it a sense of sin and prayer for forgiveness to an Almighty God. Certainly these factors are part of the basis of Christianity as we know it but this is not to say that they are part of the faith conceived of by Christ.

In worshipping God, in elevating Him to a personal and powerful figure, in asking His forgiveness, we are putting the onus on Him. Is this not a primitive, emotionally retarded and childish attitude on our part? In these days many Christians would admit that fear of God as a jealous and punishing overlord is crude and to be explained in terms of psychiatry as signifying emotional retardation. If we accept this terrified shrinking from the Father-figure as abnormal, must we not offer the same description to the undue dependence we show towards Him in asking Him to take the burden of, and the responsibility for, our sins? It would be better to accept that Christ came to take away our sense of guilt in relation to our sins, rather than to persist in the immature mechanism of laying them on the shoulders of God.

The Christian doctrine that we must pray to God for forgiveness of our sins and rely on His power and mercy to remit them for us follows directly on the Christian doctrine of grace. This is held to come from God and not to be capable of initiation by the individual. Now this leads us to a very curious anomaly. We believe that grace rests with God. We are therefore in His hands and He may withhold it from us. At the same time we believe in free will and that God endows us with liberty of choice. The Christian believes this to the degree that anything that savours of determinism has for him the taint of agnosticism and is also associated in his mind with the fatalism of the supine and degenerate East. Again, not only do we believe in freewill but the cult of the will in action is the special boast of western man. Much of our philosophy is based on the cult of the will to power. The development of our wills and the accentuation of their importance is intimately related to our morbidity and our proneness to both psychiatric and physical disease. Now all this is somewhat contradictory. We are at one and the same time utterly dependent on God's grace and at the same time fiercely insistent on the power of our own will. We insist on our freedom to choose between this and that course of action, in spite of the fact that no effort of ours can alone afford us the blessing of salvation.

Surely our emphasis on the power of our will and our right to choose is our resentful response to the doctrine that grace comes from God alone. The doctrine of grace and free will are amicably, if somewhat illogically, associated with each other on the conscious level. Translated in terms of psychiatry the one is the antagonistic response to the other. Such a curious and flagrant contradiction on the conscious level should surely be scrutinized carefully for origins in abnormal psychology.

Now what do the religions of the Far East offer by way of contrast? The general attitude of Eastern man is, or was, more submissive than our own. It is impossible to say to what extent this attitude will persist in the face of materialistic compensations offered by the West in the form of Communism or rational humanism. The present indications are that he will succumb to these alien influences. Be this as it may, in times past his submissive attitude was more basically religious than our own. We regarded those practising the Far Eastern religion as essentially will-less and fatalistic in comparison with ourselves. Yet the doctrine of Buddhism especially, and Hinduism to a less extent, is that grace essentially arises from within. According to Buddhist belief we literally reap as we have sown and our will is important in regulating our spiritual destiny. The cardinal difference between us is that with us will is more externally directed and manifests itself more in the form of personal achievements. With the Easterner the will is directed inwardly and its aim is the subjugation of personality. The manifestations of will in Western man may not necessarily result in purely materialistic or professional gains. They may involve the building up of our characters as an incident in the pursuit of material gains. At its best the construction of character may even be its primary object. But such a laudable aim is essentially conceived of as the strengthening of our personality in relation to that of others. It is not, as in the East, devoted to its annihilation.

It cannot be denied that the Eastern concept of grace and will is more realistic and healthy than our own. In building up our personalities we cannot either conquer the universe or encompass our own salvation. The use of will to subjugate our social and dynamic personalities in the face of a universe over which we have no control is an admirable solution of emotional conflict. The use of will in the limitation of personal will is the ideal prescription for the attainment of that attitude of submission which is all we can, in the last analysis, offer to the fates we cannot control.

In this section it may appear to the reader that I am writing a prescription for religion as it should be and not facing the facts of religion as they are. It may be argued that I am falling into the traditional error of seeing things as I wish them to be. Perhaps to some practitioners of psychiatry my views may be as much based on illusion as are those of the orthodox believer. On the other hand, the practising Christian may well argue that divine revelation is fixed and unalterable and not to be amended because certain features of it are inexplicable to the limited understanding of individuals. I think I have offered enough evidence to indicate that particularly for us in the West the realities of religion have been obscured and perverted by influences, chiefly ecclesiastical, which have penetrated into its substance without any true understanding of its nature. Many of the elements in present-day religion which I have found to be unacceptable and even morbid cannot in any sense be regarded as components of divine revelation. In many cases their addition to church dogma has been of comparitively recent date and has been arrived at by some approximation to the findings of a committee. Nor can I believe that items of dogma which create psychological tension can play any part in true religion. Emotional conflict which generates neurosis with all its implacable rivetting of the self within the self is the antithesis of religion. I cannot believe that what is hostile to the development of spirituality can at the same time be a pre-requisite for its inception.

Ultimately it may be that we will discover that there is one religion underlying all religions and that the Christianity, Buddhism or Hinduism we practice are merely the amended forms imposed on us by our special cultural characteristics and by the particular facts of our history. Such a view is especially repugnant to us Christians because we emphasize, to our own detriment, the especially strong historical evidence for the earthly phenomena associated with our faith. Such a conception of a religion at the core of all religions is far more acceptable to the practitioners of the Eastern faiths where the search for reality is literally a search and not something to be achieved by the acceptance of certain articles of faith.

There is considerable evidence for this persisting parent religion. The mere fact that the basic ethics of the great religions are similar is not of importance. Certain standards of behaviour must be attained if people are to live together in any state other than that of anarchy and the highest standards of conduct are often observed in those of agnostic persuasion. The golden rule is not necessarily divinely inspired and was in any case first enunciated by Confucius who could claim to be no more than a gentleman and a philosopher. What is important is that the great religions should all aim at a condition of Oneness, in which the individual seeks to be possessed and merged in a universal spirit which itself infuses all things. The separate theological systems attached to each of the great religions are merely cultural and racial additions which are to some degree inevitable and also, from the spiritual point of view, to a large extent superfluous. What I have regarded as psychiatrically undesirable features of Christianity are those malforming decorations, acquired by the religion in the course of ages, which have served to disguise its original nature.

It may be argued that even if Christianity is, in some particulars, especially conducive to neurosis, this is a fact to be accepted and that it is the lot of men to suffer. The practice of any religion, if seriously undertaken, involves a great deal of struggle and deprivation. But one must re-emphasize that the preoccupation with the integrity of the personality which is the fundamental feature of neurosis is diametrically opposed to the subjugation of personality which is the basis of true Christianity, as it is of all the other great religions. Seen from this standpoint neurosis is impiety and no person of religious inclinations can regard with satisfaction the enormous incidence of neurosis in Christian countries and, in particular, in those where the Protestant faith is dominant.

PART FOUR

Freedom and Captivity

I

SEX, SELF-ASSERTION AND SELF-ANNIHILATION

The aim of this section is to discuss the spiritual significance of sex. Since the inception of psychoanalysis, the Christian and the Freudian viewpoints on this subject have been on the whole hostile to each other. Yet these two attitudes have certain features in common. Both are only concerned with sex in relation to the social and instinctive layers of personality. They do not consider adequately its possible rôle in freeing us from the domination of our personalities and in thus facilitating the process of self-annihilation. I believe sexuality to be endowed with such a function but I recognize that its scope is limited.

I will argue in this section that sex is not the strongest of our primary urges. If it were its capacity for inducing self-annihilation would be greater than it is. The self-assertive tendency is the strongest of those primary impulses recognized both consciously by ourselves and by the philosophers and psychologists by deduction or intuition. (We have other tendencies within us far deeper than what we call our instincts but the nature of these cannot be dealt with in this book.) It is therefore necessary in this section to produce more evidence as to the strength of the self-assertive impulse. This evidence will be provided by consideration of the possibility of the existence in man of personalities other than those he recognizes as his own. If such a phenomenon is possible it testifies to the power of the self-assertive impulse because the latter is, above all, the motivating force for the construction of personality as we understand it. Until we accept the power of the self-assertive impulse we cannot appreciate the degree to which it inhibits the operations of other primary impulses such as that of sex, nor can we comprehend the obstacle it provides to the realization of self-annihilation.

We have noted previously that throughout its history Christianity has been on the whole remarkably inimical to sex. The new cult of analytic theory, though not in itself in any way an incitement to sexual licence, was, and still is, undoubtedly used as a convenient alibi by those for whom the moral conventions were particularly irksome. The Church's restrictive attitude towards sexuality was probably as much a perversion of Christ's original teaching as Freudian emancipation is a mistranslation of Freud. But we are not concerned in this section with the possible perversion of the teaching of Christ or the doctrine of Freud. What is of interest is the apparent sharp divergence of opinion on sexual matters between the Christian and the Freudian. (The definitions Christian and Freudian are over-wide and not mutually exclusive but anyone with a modest interest in either religion or psychology will recognize that till recently they represented opposing tendencies.) Of recent years there has been a considerable *rapprochement* between the parties and even the Vatican seems almost prepared to sign a concordat with what was previously regarded as a disruptive force. My aim is to show that these two divergent viewpoints had always much in common. However conflicting they may seem to have been they both arose within the confines of the egocentric personality. In the Christian attitude the inhibiting effect exercised by the social personality was uppermost. In the Freudian greater allowance was made for the expression of the instinctive forces. Neither viewpoint derived from the deep and indivisible stream of life which is below the ordinary levels of consciousness, including the subconscious, and which is potentially capable of union with the Absolute.

Neither the Christians nor the Freudians have regarded sex as an agent in the dispersal of personality. The former, inoculated more liberally with the moralizing propensities of the social personality, have held it to be a sin. The more militant Freudians,[1] leaning more to the satisfaction of the rebellious

[1] Here I am referring more to the considerable proportion of the laity influenced by ill-digested Freudianism than to the professional practitioners of psychoanalysis.

instincts, have regarded it as a right, a pleasure and an essential to health. Neither have considered it as a glimpse of the possibilities of self-annihilation. Neither have seen it as a means of release of the real Self, indivisible with life and the universe, which lies buried below and imprisoned by the two layers of personality.

We have said that the methods to be employed in order to achieve self-annihilation depend on the nature of the individual concerned. What is called physical love is one of the approaches in which sensory factors predominate. By an increasing intensity of mutual sensation two individuals achieve a climax of feeling which is, at its crescendo, an absence of personal sensation or indeed of any sensation at all. Sexual activity is the only surrender of entity commonly experienced by the average man or woman. It is a death in life and a return to the principle of Oneness which is at the basis of all religious experience. It is for this reason that love has been held for aeons to be sacred. This may seem to put too great an emphasis on what, in order to convey my meaning, I must refer to crudely as physical love. But does the marriage of mutual understanding and tolerance afford us the immense symbolism of the physical act with the implications of indivisibility? Even loving kindness, though that, too, achieves Oneness, lacks the more tremendous religious implications of the act of physical love. Any form of love is religious and tending to Oneness because feelings mutually shared render diffuse the perception of personality. Feelings unite people just as ideas separate them. But where, in ordinary human relation ships, does one lose to such a degree the sense of separate identity as one does in passionate love, even though the death which ensues from it is a very little death and its implications of Oneness very fleeting and often illusory.

I do not wish to lay any greater stress than is necessary on the importance of sexual activity. The emphasis on crude sex at the present day is most undesirable, though its harmful effects cannot be compared with those induced by the repression exercised by Victorian morality. If I seem to lend to human passion a greater dignity than it merits, I should make it quite clear that I consider that acts of love motivated simply and solely by the sexual urges are probably unknown. It is impossible to conceive of love as consisting purely and simply of physical desire. If such a thing were possible it would not be a coarse and animal rite but something of great purity and sanctity, the dignity of which would be enhanced by its purely sensual nature.[2] But most sexual intercourse, even that within the confines of wedlock and between those who love each other, is contaminated by the urge to dominate, either by taking and possessing in the case of the male, or by the exercise of seduction in that of the female. He who is conscious of taking a woman as his own may experience an even delirious pleasure, but this is not sexual experience in the strict sense of the word but a power-engendered joy in possession with the added pleasure of partial sexual titillation. The dominating motive in the lives of the libertine and the harlot is not sexuality but power. This is not surprising because the desire for power over others is the predominating human motive. In the will to power desire for domination very often outruns performance. Not all are sufficiently talented to be leaders of men and not all sufficiently unscrupulous to be Napoleons of finance. But all individuals, except the lowest forms of ament, are endowed with sexual instincts. This is of all human attributes the most readily available, to the gifted and ungifted, to the spiritually and the materially minded, for exercising their dominion over others.

One can discover this exercise of the power motive by the most cursory scrutiny of one's married acquaintances. How often do we see the weak and dependent male attached to the dominating and carnivorous female by the thin thread of a half-forced sexuality on the part of the woman? How often do we encounter the brainless and vapid wife holding an intelligent and relatively unassertive male by the licensed harlotry of her conception of wedlock? How often does the timid, submissive and delicate wife possess and discipline her human gorilla by the magnet of a sexuality dressed out in the garments of helpless innocence? If we observe carefully we will see how many marriages are based on the principle that opposing forces

[2] This is because such passion, if it could be achieved, would be all-consuming. This latter is the adjective applied to it in romantic novels. Such a state is seldom achieved and if the novelist imagines it to be, he or she is for the most part incapable of interpreting its religious nature. Passion which is consuming devours the self, that is to say the false self, of the human personality. From our observation of our fellows we can see that this is seldom achieved, though sexual activity must be not uncommon.

are complementary to each other and make, when joined together, some kind of whole. In a few cases, which perhaps we can describe as those marriages made in heaven, the man and woman are lost in each other and the marriage is an experience of oneness and of the nature of a sacrament. But for the most part such complementary relationships are balances of forces in which for the purposes of domination the weak utilize their weakness and the strong their strength.

A digression is necessary here because the statement that the urge to power is the strongest of all human motives needs amplification. This urge to power is a manifestation of the self-assertive instinctive which is the chief motivating force in the construction of personality. I cannot see how we can deny that the urge to power is the strongest of man's innate impulses if we consider that the possession of personality which so largely derives from it is the attribute which demarcates man most sharply from other forms of creation. This is not to say that animals do not possess personality. The idea that the Creator prescribed personality as a kind of injection to distinguish man from his fellow creatures is something too ingenuous to contemplate. The influence which impregnates the universe is not given to proceeding in bounds like a kangaroo, though the degree to which theologians jump to conclusions would almost lead one to believe that they were emulating some form of celestial acrobatics. But in other forms of creation the personality is vague and shadowy and only recognisable at all in those few domestic animals which live in close contact with man. The possession of personality endows man with a subjectively perceived apartness which has no counterpart in animal creation. He is separated from his fellows to a greater degree than an animal from other members of the herd by the multiplicity of aims and desires expressed in his personality. His will to power is infinite because his existence is so intricately competitive. An animal kills to eat, to withstand the menace of hostile species and to establish himself as the lord of the jungle. Such motives are of crystalline simplicity compared with the power urges which govern human beings. The animals which have accepted the dominion of the lord of the jungle cease to challenge it until the king in his turn is old, stricken and easily despatched. But the possession of personality makes each man a lord in his own right and the form in which he exercises his authority depends for the most part on his nature and accomplishments. He may exercise his power by physical force, by the coercion of systems of ideas, or by symptoms of disease subtly produced to afford him his place in the sun.

One of Freud's most cardinal errors was to regard the sexual instinct as the strongest of man's hereditary acquisitions. Perhaps one cannot dispute that it is the primary factor in his instinctual equipment. One can concede this to be possible in that a species to endure must be endowed with the capacity to propagate itself. One can accept all that Freud says on the subject of infantile experience without amending one's view that the power motive, or self-assertive instinct, is the strongest of human urges. The fact that the sexual impulse is the most basic element of man's instinctual equipment and the earliest to be manifested does not necessarily indicate that it remains throughout his life the strongest force of his dynamic personality. In addition, it is doubtful whether we can accept any longer the psycho-analytical doctrine that only instincts and not personality traits can be inherited. We see too many individuals growing up too closely to the pattern of one or other parent to accept with easy minds the Freudian view that such characteristics are acquired as the results of environmental influences. It is quite easy to accept that the persistence of obsessional characteristics throughout several generations is conditioned by the repetition of environmental influence. It is a little fantastic to use the same explanation for the transmission of incidental gestures or minor peculiarities of gait not attributable to physical malformations or to imitation.

If we accept the Jungian doctrine of the racial unconscious we must consider possible the inheritance of personality traits because the racial unconscious requires the vehicle of pre-existing human personality for its transmission. Nor can we dismiss as fanciful the phenomenon of backward remembering of previous existences. We may not like the doctrine of reincarnation but, if we consider the whole world and the whole course of recorded time, the thinkers and prophets who have believed in reincarnation are an impressive company. We should not dismiss such doctrines as fanciful because they do not accord with Western ideas. Except for a few mystics we in the West have not shown ourselves especially adept in dispersing ourselves through time. Nor are we likely to do so if we maintain our obsessive preoccupation with our own personalities, because the concept of personality is closely related to the mathematical computation of time, whereas, for the mystic, the experience of reality invariably carries with it an impression of timelessness and of the primodial and real Self being diffused through time and space.

There is evidence that some individuals have the power of recalling to some extent pre-existing personalities the memories of which still operate within them. The distinguished novelist, Joan Grant, has written books on ancient Greece, ancient Egypt and mediaeval Italy. She has been complimented by classicists, Egyptologists and historians on her remarkably accurate knowledge of the three above-mentioned cultures of which she has written. She received what, for a woman, was an education unusually biased in the direction of mathematics and the natural sciences. She certainly received no education such as would provide her with the data necessary for the composition of her books. It is difficult to explain such phenomena unless we regard them as evidence of backward remembering. We may take the materialistic view that this author's gifts are to be attributed to some psychopathological peculiarity, say, to hysterical dissocation. This involves us in the necessity of stating the particular psychiatric infirmity which permits us to produce accurately and to the satisfaction of scholars a coherent and valid picture of life in distant times. There is no such malady. Can we fall back on Jung's teaching and say that the example quoted above is merely an accentuated form of the racial unconscious erupting at the conscious level? No, because here we have an example of highly selective recollection such as could only be attributed to the agency of a coherent personality. Also the recollection reaches the conscious level. The racial unconscious is formless, in our meaning of the term, and exists below the conscious level of the individual. Most important of all it expresses itself in symbols and not in direct recollections.

In relation to this question of pre-existing personalities one further point can be made. Whatever chain of causes underlies schizophrenia I feel that the remarkably incoherent behaviour and speech of the schizophrenic, and his swift and entirely irrelevant change from one line of thought or action to another indicate to some extent the effects of a confusion of personalities within the patient. Perhaps these lightning variations of behaviour are best exemplified by considering with what speed a patient may pass from a condition of catatonic stupor to one of catatonic excitement. In the former condition the patient may be inert, stuporose and unseeing, dribbling saliva and indifferent to the calls of nature. This may go on for days or weeks and may be terminated with dramatic rapidity by a quite sudden and pointless attack on the person nearest to him. It is almost as though he were another person. One wonders whether this latter description, which could be applied to the patient by any untutored observer, contains an element of truth. A similar phenomenon is presented by the brutal and pointless acts of violence committed on a sudden by a small proportion of epileptics. One moment the patient is a whining and religiose hypochondriac. The next he is battering some incidental passer-by to pieces. It is easy to conceive of biochemical factors at work in the case of the catatonic schizophrenic and the epileptic. Noxious chemicals accumulate in the blood and at the flash point the cerebral cortex erupts volcanically. One can understand that a convulsion could result from such sudden cerebral stimulation but why a coherent though alarmingly unexpected pattern of behaviour during a few seconds or minutes detached from the rest of existence? It is also difficult to conceive of a special centre in the brain for the smashing of the heads of strangers with cudgels.

If we search for an explanation in terms of current psychiatry our task is still difficult. We know that extreme and pathological variations of mood can occur in the same individual. In those of manic-depressive constitution the individual in the depressed phase is depressed, self-accusatory and hyper-conscientious. In the manic phase he is elated, arrogantly self-conscious and, so far as conscientiousness is concerned, too grandiose to consider seriously his social obligations. The pattern of behaviour exhibited in the two phases of the disease is totally different but one would hesitate to say that it is as though two persons existed in the same individual because the two natures exhibited are too neatly and accurately opposed to each other. Each is the reverse side of the same medal. The change from one state to another may be slow and may be conducted across a gulf of normality, so that we may not be inclined to believe that we are confronted with the spectacle of one personality ousting another. On the other hand, the change may be rapid and the patient may pass in the course of a day from arrogant elation to self-accusing depression. But in the true manic-depressive condition we do not get isolated, brief and dramatic episodes inserted into whichever phase of depression or elation is uppermost. The melancholic does not burst into two minutes mania and then subside again. We cannot, then, wholly explain the fragmentary violence of the epileptic or the sudden impulsiveness of the patient previously in a catatonic stupor in terms of such a constitutional factor as exists in the manic-depressive psychosis.

If we try to explain such brief catastrophic symptoms in terms of modern psychiatry with Freudian analysis as its basis we are confronted with considerable difficulties. In mild versions of the manic-depressive state, where the condition does not amount to a mental disease, we might describe the elation and self-confidence of the manic phase as a process of wish-fulfilment germinating but unexpressed during the depressed phase. Can we apply such an explanation to the case of the epileptic boiling up into his brief episode of pointless violence? The Freudian would say that this might be an expression of the death wish and one hesitates to say that this view is wrong. But in the present state of knowledge we must point out that the constitutional factor is uppermost in epilepsy. The idiopathic version of the disease carries with it very often stigmata of degeneration which have been present during the whole lifetime of the patient. The peculiar skin and oddly flat voice of the epileptic are characteristic features which, though not invariable, are very commonly present in the variety of epileptics doomed to deterioration. It is precisely because there is a constitutional element in this disease that it is so difficult to explain the outbreaks of violence purely in terms of constitutional factors confined within the limited biology of the patient's own lifetime. It may be argued that epileptics are notoriously irritable people and quick to take offence, but this is to beg the question because irritability is a feature in many psychiatric disorders and the characteristic symptom of the epileptic crime is its utterly pointless victimization of persons who have not insulted the patient. (It should be made clear that these attacks are not, as in the case of paranoid patients, the result of delusions.)

But if the reader prefers to regard the epileptic crime as the end point of epileptic irritability let us return again to the case of the schizophrenic. The essential feature of schizophrenia is apathy and complete loss of interest in the environment. Why then these sudden attacks on neutrals? Is this, in terms of psychoanalytic theory, a sudden attempt to establish *rapport* with his environment? Perhaps, but such an explanation involves us in the anomaly that such an attempt occurs in individuals in whom the social personality is almost extinct. Emotional conflict occurs when the aims of the social and instinctive personalities are divergent. Why should there be conflict in a person where the social personality has abdicated to the degree that the patient is drooling and incontinent?

In former ages epileptics were regarded as possessed. It is not difficult to envisage that such explanations were also offered to account for the phenomenon of sudden violence in the patient previously in a state of catatonic stupor. Possessed meant possession by the Devil. Are we then reverting to mediaeval doctrine to explain these phenomena? On no account, but we should consider that it is possible that these signs and symptoms can be the brief eruption of pre-existing personalities in the individual. Of all psychiatric diseases schizophrenia is, in its delusional content, the richest in that form of symbolism which is the expression of the racial unconscious. If we accept that this conception of Jung's is valid it is not too much to suppose that in some cases, interspersed amid the formlessness of the racial unconscious, there are the shadows of pre-existing personalities. If we accept that we are influenced by the emotional content of our spiritual ancestry, it is possible to envisage that in some patients there exist more coherent and shadowy reaction patterns which are the residue within them of previous personalities.

I have laboured this point of pre-existing personalities in order to demonstrate that the self-assertive instinct, which manifests itself in the will to power, and which is the principal motivating force of personality, is the strongest of our human instinctive acquisitions. Power is the aim and the will to power the weapon of that personality, fabricated from the social and dynamic aspects of our nature, which, in the course of life, we manufacture for ourselves from the essence of which we are made. The evidence that the self-assertive instinct is the strongest of all is weighty enough without postulating the existence of pre-personalities within us. If this latter concept can be accepted the evidence becomes still stronger. The reason why we are at present loath to accept it is because we are too influenced by the Freudian doctrine which attributes altogether too much to our immediate familial environment. I do not see how we can accept the principle of hereditary factors in so-called physical diseases like tuberculosis, if we do not extend this conception to cover our psychiatric equipment. The human personality acts and reacts as a total entity. Disease is a more or less localized expression of total personality in conflict with total environment. If tuberculosis is part of the total reaction of a human personality, and if we concede that there is, in this disease, a strong hereditary factor, then we must also admit, on the principle that the greater includes the less, that the personality of which the disease is the expression is also to some degree inherited. We must, of course, always allow that the form in which the personality expresses itself can be considerably modified by the environment or by the individual's reaction to it.

The reader may deduce from these remarks that I am stating a set of contentions the practical application of which would amount to therapeutic nihilism. If personalities, with all their physical and psychiatric flaws, are inherited, what is the ultimate usefulness of treatment and are we, so far as our more resistant chronic maladies are concerned, struggling in a morass from which we cannot extricate ourselves? The present answer must be yes. We will suffer from the diseases of personality so long as we emphasize the importance of personality. With the eyes of vision so closely on ourselves we will continue to discover our morbid symptoms. The answer to our medical problems is the answer to our spiritual problems. Until we succeed in freeing from the shackles of personality our real selves, independent of our personalities but contiguous with the mainstream of consciousness, we will be prone to those diseases which, at the moment, most commonly affect us. What we are suffering from is decay in the walls which we ourselves have built around us. Psycho-analytic teaching has revealed to us how man clings to his symptoms and how with only a part of his nature is he willing to surrender them. The truth can be expressed more simply than in the nomenclature of the Vienna School. We cannot shed our symptoms because we cannot shed ourselves.

The self-assertive and the sexual instincts accompany us throughout our lives but each runs its race at a different pace and neither adheres to the principle of equal times for each lap. We cannot escape from the fact that the climate of infancy is overwhelmingly sexual. The infant lives in a simple, erotic world, the sexuality of which is only shadowy to those whose conception of sex is limited to acts of intercourse and their related variants. As the child is separated gradually from an atmosphere more or less exclusively provided by its mother its world is less completely sexual. In the child's early schooldays the development of the self-assertive instinct becomes more manifest, but with the onset of puberty the sexual instinct makes its next bid for obvious and conscious domination. By this time, however, the reinvigorated sex instinct is acting against the background of heightened self-assertive impulses in a personality infinitely more coherent than that of the infant or child of primary school age. In the vast majority of modern adults this reinvigorated instinct is a perpetual and aggressive nuisance. It is often no more than a weapon of self-assertion expressing itself through sexual channels.

We have said that in its infancy the child lives in an almost exclusively sexual climate. Its life is to a considerable extent contiguous with that of its mother. It feeds at her breast and constantly receives from her intimate attentions. In its early infancy it achieves a degree of oneness with its mother greater than any it is ever likely to achieve again with any other individual. Its personality is unformed and it is still to a large extent merged in another. This relative continuousness with its mother is chiefly conducted across the bridge of its erotic feelings. It is true that there is the primitive urge of hunger to be considered, but the ingestion of food, and therefore the child's very existence, is conducted through the medium of erotic sensation. The child sucks at its mother's breast and the satisfaction both derive from the process is obvious. The human individual is probably more fulfilled sexually in infancy than at any other period of his existence. Even if he develops into a complete libertine episodic seductions, however frequent, can never achieve the erotic intensity which existed in the first months of his life and which was associated, in the act of suckling, with the very maintenance of his existence. Many adults are libertines not because the sex act is the only thing in life which really satisfies them but because it is of all things that which leaves them most unsatisfied. How often is this constantly unfilled and almost deterministic career of libertinism a search through many women for the one woman, his mother, with whom, through the medium of erotic factors, he obtained peace and oneness. The infant, then, enjoys his most complete sexuality at that period of his existence when he is most innocent.

I have laboured this association of a predominantly erotic existence and the age of innocence in order to reinforce my previous point that pure sexuality, unaccompanied by the power motive, may be a means of attaining, in adult life, the sense of oneness and the abandonment of personality which are primary elements of religious experience. Now here we begin to obtain a glimpse of the reason for the antipathy of Christian clericalism to sexuality. The ecclesiastical mentality, in its worship of set forms and in its insistence on expiatory rituals, is, when confronted with sexuality, only concerned with what it considers a sin unless its practice has previously been hallowed by wedlock. The Anglican marriage service leave us in no doubt where we stand in this matter. Young love may be a transforming and even an ethereal experience but, in the eyes of the Church, the sexual feelings which accompany it are essentially an impulse to fornication, a rather meaningless word which indicates the dire significance placed by the Church on a natural impulse. The latter is essentially sinful unless it is transformed into something holy in the space of quarter of an hour by a set form of address enunciated by a fallible human being. The Church service is at one and the same time a cleansing ritual for something which alone and of itself was never unclean and a piece of canned sexuality which is a result of the obsessive preoccupation of clericalism with these matters. Throughout the ages organized Christianity has mistrusted and persecuted those manifestations of mystical experience without which the forms of religion are merely systems of ethics with a binding fabric of superstition and neurosis. For some sexual love is a key to mystical experience because the merging of one with another involves a personal though fleeting death. Now those for whom sexual activity can act as such a key are relatively few. It is not what sex brings to man but what man brings to sex which is of importance. For the vast majority sex is a pleasant appetite, a delirious and misleading joy, or a coarse gluttony. It is, in fact, a form of self-indulgence. It is only for the very few that it holds possibilities of self-annihilation. Nevertheless it is sufficiently recognized that sex can be a form of escape from the personality for it to be mistrusted by the exponents of clericalism.

It must not be deduced from this that throughout the centuries clericalism has been totally opposed to the religious principle of self-annihilation. Certainly its opposition has been remarkably constant and often fierce. The Church's persecution of its own mystics, often conveniently libelled as heretics, is sufficient evidence. But where the Church has recognized that self-annihilation is the basis of religious experience it has, in virtue of its sin of sectarianism, insisted too often on dictating the channels through which this impulse must express itself. The individual losing himself to the world and finding himself by the agency of sexual experience is altogether too slippery a customer to be allowed to escape unindicted. The very ubiquitousness of the sexual impulse is enough to make clericalism afraid of it. Anybody, any ordinary animal man, might find himself in virtue of his animal endowments a little closer to God. The idea that perhaps hundreds of thousands may experience, in a few moments of bliss, the presence of God, without the formulation of set beliefs and without the utilization of what the Church has understood by faith, is anathema to the well-organized and well-disciplined religiosity which has masqueraded as Christianity to this day. Clericalism has achieved much in closing the sexual channel to spiritual experience. It has impregnated sexuality with so much guilt that the act of love is approached with a greater self-consciousness than it need be. This self-consciousness is no better and may even be worse in those who resist the authority of the Church because a sense of resistance is itself self-conscious.

The clerical attitude to women is inextricably bound up with its attitude to sexuality. We have on the one hand Christ, Incarnate of the Virgin Mary, who preached a doctrine which may be roughly summarized as the elevation of the female virtues in a world dominated by the masculine vices. We have on the other the Church which has at different periods of its history regarded women as the agents of the Devil and has at one period given illuminatory testimony to its own state of mind by referring to them as the Sex. This attitude dies hard. A friend of mine in a pre-war Polish school was instructed by a priest that women were sent on earth to tempt man. A recent conference of Anglicans was opposed to women being ordained and expressed itself on the subject with clowning infantilism. The idea of such a proposition ever being made in the Roman Church is unthinkable. Presumably these men had mothers but it seems that for different reasons they are unable to contemplate without revulsion any simulacrum of the state of erotic innocence in which they lived in the first months of their lives. It is characteristic of all great religions that they insist on the necessity for rebirth. It is too wide a subject for one to embark here on the degree to which spiritual rebirth implies a return to the indifferentiated life of childhood before the formation of personality. To be reborn does not, of course, imply a return to an erotic attitude towards life but it envisages a re-entry into that phase of existence when erotic factors were uppermost in consciousness. And this is the period of life when the child lived its existence not dependent on itself but within the orbit of woman. The man-woman relationship conducted on a purely sexual basis—it cannot exist but the Church thinks it can—would be essentially, in religious terms, the repetition in adult life of the child-mother relationship. It is not surprising that the symbol of a truly religious experience should be condemned by the exponents of an organized religiosity.

Yet in spite of it all the Roman Church has beatified the Virgin Mary. I do not think this is a contradictory attitude. The

Church is sanctifying the Virgin and not Mary. Virginity withholds from man the possibilities of the world-losing act which gives him a few second's intimation of a higher existence. The worship of the physical conception of virginity and chastity has been part of the stock in trade of clericalism throughout the centuries. It is another example of the ecclesiastical preoccupation with external forms. But blessed are the pure in heart, and within the limits of our human understanding, this must mean those who seek God and abandon themselves in so doing and it is even possible that some may attain to this by physical passion.

I have dealt with what I consider to be the reasons for the Church's attitude towards sexuality. I do not think I need devote much space to any further discussion of the Freudian standpoint. The latter is merely provoked by the former. It is its direct antithesis and therefore of the same nature. We are too slow to learn that opposites have a common origin and that to escape from error it is not necessary for us to react in opposite directions but to transport ourselves to different planes of reaction. Both Freudian freedom and clerical restriction are conducted against a background of intense belief in the importance of personality in the egotistical sense of the term. The clerical attitude arises mainly from the moralizing strata, the Freudian from the rebellious, instinctive layers of being. Under their aegis sex can only serve to heighten the assertive personality's consciousness of itself. No man was ever made whole by following crude pseudo-scientific exhortations to have a woman. To have is to possess and to seek to possess is to forego what opportunities sex affords for the dissolution of personality. That is the importance of love, that, where it exists, sex is merely the instrument of a total tendency on the part of the whole individual to lose itself in another. Feelings of self-gratification, triumph and a sense of spurious maturity are all obstacles to the experience of reality which can be attained in sexual love. Exhortations to abstinence, when these derive from the negative motives of morality, are equally unfruitful. A resentful and hollow self-consciousness is no more spiritual than the self-satisfaction of gluttony.

Reading of the gospels reveals that Christ did not offer a great deal of positive guidance in the matter of sex. This is not a weakness in His teaching but part of its strength. The physical gratification of the sex impulse is an important part of life but the elevation of intercourse to the level of a primary necessity is one of the most tedious aspects of our garish, shallow and dull-witted civilization. But it should not be deduced that Christ deliberately minimised the importance of the sexual impulse. His attitude was of tolerance towards it as, for example, in the case of the woman discovered in adultery. If we ask ourselves what is the function of sex interpreted in the light of Christ's teaching our best answer is that we should not consider sex as a separate impulse. We must ponder to what extent it facilitates or impedes the harmony of the whole man. If physical desire prevents a man suitably constituted from living more fully a dedicated life, whether this life be devoted to contemplation or action, then it is to be deprecated. If, on the other hand, it enables those poorly endowed for the realities of religious experience to gain a momentary glimpse of the universality of all things then it can only be regarded as good. On the whole the great prophets have avoided specific exhortations and prohibitions in relation to sex. These latter have been the especial stock-in-trade of the strait-laced moralists, spiritually impoverished and devoid of charity, who have so regularly perverted and mummified the truths bequeathed to them by those who have gone before.

When we are discussing sex we should realize that the ultimate spiritual disaster is apartness as the ultimate spiritual goal is oneness. According to the book of Genesis God created Adam, a man, in His own image. This implies that man was continuous in nature with God and shared His Divinity. Then followed the creation of Eve and afterwards the consumption of the fruit of the tree of knowledge. At first our original ancestors were naked and not ashamed but following their ingestion of the forbidden fruit they adopted garments in an effort to hide their separate identity. This measure served only to accentuate the differences between them. It would be altogether too naïve to connect directly the imponderables of good and evil with the mere phenomenon of their sexual differences. The sin of Adam and Eve was surely that each built round his or her separate physical identity a set of values which were no longer immediately dependent on direct contact with God. Their sin, indeed, was the sin of schism. When God debarred them from eating of the tree of knowledge of good and evil He was not putting on them any unjust or impossible embargo to impede their investigation of the nature of ethics. They themselves created good and evil by separating themselves from God. The bitter fruit of the tree of knowledge was the bane of separate personality. Both man and woman acquired for themselves a distinctive psychology and a distinctive standard of values. These acquisitions not only emphasized their own apartness but involved their separation from God.

In the Old Testament allegory the birth of sin lies not in the separate sexuality of Adam and Eve but in the separate natures they built around it. With each step towards separate identity they moved farther away from God. That they hid their sexual organs by fig leaves implies, in the terms of the allegory, not that they were hiding from each other but that both were hiding from Him. That the sin lay not in the separate sexuality itself is revealed in the allegory by the words 'And Adam said, This is now bone of my bones and flesh of my flesh', and later, 'Therefore shall a man leave his father and his mother and shall cleave unto his wife, and they shall be one flesh'. The whole implication is that sin lies not in the separate nature of sex nor in the act of fusion. It lies in the fact that the allegory uses the terms man and woman as the most striking example of separate personalities which it would be possible to offer.

The story of Genesis outlines for us the sin of apartness. It stresses also that sexuality was not a sin but an insurance against apartness. 'They shall be as one flesh'. Yet the accent of clericalism has always been on the sin of sexuality as such. The male, aggressive and sometimes homosexual component in clericalism has always been hostile to the symbolic self-annihilation implied in the sexual act. It is a strange commentary on organized religion that it should, on the whole, have been so inimical to the one act common to mankind which symbolizes the return to oneness and to communion with the Infinite.

The strange feature about the Old Testament story of Adam is that man is mentioned as the first representative of the human species. Other religious systems of the world have instead the concept of the Great Mother. This latter would seem to be more logical in that human lives do, after all, begin within her and are developed from her. Is the story of Adam a primarily Semitic concept and does it express the dominance of the more aggressive male principle? Was the doctrine of Christ the return to the concept of the primary importance and the greater sanctity of the woman principle? Christ's doctrine was, after all, the embodiment of the female virtues of pity and mercy. It was certainly a protest against the Jewish conception of religion, a concept which is still paramount in organized Christianity to a degree which is obvious to any one who studies it with reasonable care.

The doctrine of the Immaculate Conception indicates that the male sex was specifically excluded from partaking in the birth of Christ. The woman and the child express the same idea of a continuum as do the woman and man when joined in love but they do so more tangibly and over a longer period of time.

If sex, either in actual physical practice, or as a source of energy in the form of sublimation, is to have any spiritual significance, it must express itself as an agent of self- annihilation and as an aspiration to oneness. Where it is dragged at the wheel of the instinctive personality it makes more coherent the fabric of personality but is ultimately disruptive, as is everything which man acquires in feeding his self-esteem. If the Church had limited itself to the condemnation of sexuality as a self-indulgence all would have been well. That it has so consistently and for so long indicted sex as a whole, except for the purposes of procreation, indicates to what degree it has failed to appreciate that it can be a catylst in self-obliteration and therefore an activity of potentially spiritual value.

In concluding this chapter one should mention another important aspect of human sexual relationships. Christianity has always stressed not only the sanctity of marriage but the principle that the love of a man for his wife is all absorbing and should exclude all passion which has other women as its object. At the same time Christianity has, on the whole, in relation to the other great religions, afforded to women a greater degree of equality and a greater spiritual significance. The position of women in Mohammedan communities is certainly not so favourable seen by the above standards. It can, too, hardly be denied that, again by our standards, the lot of women, till recently at any rate, has been less happy in Buddhist and Hindu communities. There can be no doubt that our attitude is more desirable on the grounds of social justice and common humanity but it has its dangers. It is a matter of common experience, whether we like it or not, that some of those of promiscuous inclinations exhibit in other respects more of the Christian virtues than do the eminently respectable. It may be that this is because their more complete sensuous satisfaction dilutes the urges to power and self-assertion and endows them with greater charity and tolerance. I hesitate to advance this view because it can only apply to a few and because so much libertinism is more an expression of self-assertion than sexuality. A more important factor, from the spiritual point of view, is that the promiscuous may be less obsessive in their love than those whose passion is expended on one woman only. It may be that the woman in question cannot, in the act of love, provide her husband with the key to a spiritual experience however insubstantial and fragmentary. This being so, the very fact that his religious code renders this his sole opportunity may be stultifying from the standpoint of the individual for whom physical love provides the only tangible possibility of self-annihilation. Again, the knowledge that he is limited to one woman may further incline him to fail. All this is not to be translated as an argument in favour of unorganized promiscuousness or, worse still, the sad, mechanized futilities of free love and trial marriage. All one is saying is that an excessive preoccupation with the spiritual potentialities of marriage may actually lead to their reduction. So often in life too positive aims produce negative results.

Finally it should be remembered that according to the marriage service this institution exists for the procreation, without sin, of children. The liturgy clearly excludes from consideration the possibility that physical love may be itself uplifting. Intercourse outside marriage is fornication. Within the bounds of wedlock it is sinless but is not credited with positive merits.

The sanctification of human love, of one man for one woman, may go too far from the spiritual point of view. It is well enough if, in the act of love, the participants obtain glimpses of the infinite. On the other hand the over-sanctification of the married state may be a bar to spiritual development. Christians often shrink from what appear to them Christ's relatively cold references to His earthly family. We should consider it possible that the implication of what He said on these occasions is that to be too absorbed in any human tie may prevent men from attaining the maximum spiritual development otherwise possible to them.

If a man's only glimpse of a higher life is to be obtained through a woman then it is a happy circumstance that they should marry and devote themselves to each other. If, however, either partner has a latent capacity for spiritual development independent of such a relationship as marriage, then the fact should be faced that the latter institution may from this point of view be restrictive.

I think that in its great emphasis on the sanctity of marriage the Church may well have erred. Certainly it is right socially. It may be wrong spiritually. In its fear of sexuality as a whole the Christian church may have made, as an effort of compensation, a cardinal error in overemphasizing the virtues of the licensed sexuality experienced in marriage. Of course it may be that Christianity differs from Buddhism and Hinduism in its greater emphasis on such human relationships. Certainly we prefer to believe it so because it suits our natures to do so. But in the face of certain passages in the Gospels which are disturbing to us, I feel that we may well have modified original Christian teaching to suit our own predilections. There are so many likenesses in the psychological foundations of the great religions that we should hesitate before claiming for our own a unique preoccupation with human relationships.

II

CURRENT ERRORS IN PSYCHIATRIC TREATMENT

It might now be profitable to discuss some of the current errors in psychiatric treatment. We will only consider those which stand in relation to our central theme of psychiatry and religion. Possibly the most erroneous tendency in treatment is the psychiatrist's almost automatic preoccupation with the patient's possibilities of self-expression. Inquiries as to the latter's aspirations, ambitions, creative impulses and hobbies are almost routine. This is very praiseworthy where the enquiry is pursued to enable the psychiatrist to obtain a clear picture of the patient. Where it is used as a basis for treatment the results are not so happy. This is seen very often in those cases where the patient it urged to take up a hobby or to express himself in one or other of the forms of art. Now there is considerable evidence that frustration of the creative impulses is one of the factors conducive to development of neurosis. But if the individual has had a strong impulse to see things grow under his own hand it is more than likely that he will have already become a gardener. There is a whole world of difference between this and being advised by a psychiatrist to take up such a pastime. In the former case the individual has already embarked on what he loves doing. He is, in fact, working as much or more for the garden as for himself. The patient, on the other hand, is merely being urged towards an artificial and self-conscious method of self-expression. In the former case the individual is lost in what he loves doing. The burden of personality is shed. In the latter he continues in a state of uncomfortable awareness of his self and hopes that the desirable obliteration of personality will somehow result from it.

The psychiatrist is often reduced to the prescription of such superficial methods of treatment because of the inadequate time at his disposal. Little harm is done if he limits himself to the recommendation of hobbies and interests for those conspicuously lacking in them. When, however, he becomes obsessed by the desire to avoid his patient being frustrated, there is no end to the harm which he can do. Injudicious advice as to the changing of jobs is a potent source of error. In extreme cases patients are advised to abandon safe and mundane occupations for speculative and colourful adventures in the creative arts. We are not all Hartnells or Sprys and still less Monets and Shelleys. It should be remembered that the creative urge is often spurious and engendered by the neurotic's desire to compensate for his own inadequacy. Too little effort is made to encourage the patient to accept what, according to worldly standards, must be the lot of the vast majority. These attempts to stimulate him to greater self-expression merely increase his evaluation of the over-assertive personality which is responsible for his condition. Since the basis of religious experience is submission and since this offers the human being his best hope of serenity, it seems a pity that the psychiatrist's efforts should be wasted in exhortations which engulf the patient further in the morass of competitive existence. Such forms of therapy reflect that the psychiatrist himself is a victim of the materialistic philosophy which insists that there is something healthy, and possibly holy, in furthering the excesses of our over-assertive and acquisitive personalities. These panaceas for frustration may afford temporary relief but they are in themselves sources of further danger seeing that, under their aegis, the patient is led still further down the blind alleys of self-expression.

The value of any sort of vocational guidance depends not on the degree to which it facilitates directly the individual's capacity to express himself but on the extent to which it permits him to achieve self-annihilation. He may attain this latter desirable condition by psychiatric treatment. If he does so it is because therapy frees him from his conflicts and releases spiritual energies which pour themselves along channels hitherto barred to them. Such results are never achieved by direct exhortation on the part of the psychiatrist.

This form of therapy which insists on self-expression on the conscious level is of wide range. It includes a good deal of the advice given as to increased social activity or the devotion of oneself to public work. The latter can be a particularly disastrous form of advice not only because it may not improve tangibly the patient's condition but because it may prove positively disadvantageous to the community. The political scene, both national and local, is surely sufficiently contaminated with power-addicts without further recruits being enrolled on the recommendation of the psychiatrist. With regard to ordinary social relationships, it cannot be denied that occasional conviviality with our fellows is good for most of us. We should, however, remember Pascal's dictum that the sum total of human misery is due to man's inability to remain happy within four walls. It is also axiomatic that there is no guarantee of serenity in the flux and chance of human relationships. Paradoxically enough, those whose thoughts are turned to the

Absolute may derive from human relationships more happiness than does the average individual. Their contact with their fellows is conducted with a lighter touch. Certainly one should not despise the ease and comfort which we derive from gregarious activities. Few of us are so spiritually endowed that we can afford to forego what we derive from our friends and acquaintances. We should remember, however, that when in the throes of neurosis we transport to our acquaintances the selves of which we are over-conscious in the hope that in their company our stresses will be resolved, we are availing ourselves of a drug. It is certainly among the best of drugs and drugs are by no means to be despised. We should not, however, delude ourselves that our fundamental condition is radically amended by such activities and we should remember that in age and near death we become increasingly alone.

Injudicious treatment based on the attitude that frustration must be avoided at all costs is quite deadly. Because the Freudian theory pointed out that certain neurotic symptoms can result from the suppression of the primary urges, it has been too widely assumed that the solution is simply to express the instinctive impulses as much as possible. This is lamentably crude. The wholesale expression of instinctive impulses brings the patient in conflict with the moral code of society and so provides him with fresh problems. Worse still, it leaves undisturbed the fundamental basis of his malady. The situation is nowadays worse than in pre-Freudian days because the removal of the inhibitions makes individuals still more the slaves of their impulses.[3] We should admit with Freud that intense repression of the sexual instinct may result in neurotic symptoms. Nevertheless the near-sanctification of this, or other instincts, is in the long run equally or even more harmful. What happens to the individual who has made a god of his instincts when these latter begin to wane? In assessing these factors we should remember that the incidence of neurosis has increased since the age of Freud. Naturally there are many reasons for

[3] When I speak of men being the slaves of their impulses it should be remembered that to be wholly given to an impulse is one of the forms of self-obliteration and may therefore be of benefit. It should be remembered, however, that instinctive impulses such as that of sex are seldom, if ever, exhibited in their pure form and are practically always contaminated by self-assertion and the will to power.

this and perhaps the chief among them is that when neurosis became socially permissible its future was assured. Still, the increase in this type of malady following the dissemination of Freudian doctrine needs careful consideration.

Psychiatry has not faced the fact that the limitation of the scope of personality rather than its increased expression is the key to peace. I know of no Western school of psychiatry which advocates the diminution of the potential of personality by the reduction of its instinctive urges. I use the word reduction rather than control because the latter implies the discipline inflicted on the dynamic by the social personality. This has always occurred and is responsible for the process of repression which results in our accentuation of neurotic tendencies. The reduction of the power of the instinctive personality can only be achieved by techniques of contemplation, self-analysis and relaxation dedicated to the aim of seeing oneself as a unit of life separated off from the main stream of existence by the malforming illusion of personality. Until we have learnt to see ourselves as nothing we will never liberate the real self which is buried below not only our social but our instinctive personality. Such aims and techniques may be practised under the aegis of religion or outside the confines of organized psychiatry. They play no part in psychiatry as practised in the medical profession.

In America we see the dead opposite of this desirable negation of personality. In that country there is a copious literature devoted to the relief of neurotic symptoms. Much of it involves the encouragement of what is called positive thinking. The patient is encouraged to go out and buy a new hat because God wishes her to do so. It is gratifying to discover that as a result of such methods of treatment the patient as often as not finds him or herself more successful and prosperous than before. It is only to be expected of a nation obsessed by achievement that the cult of success should be incorporated in its therapeutic and religious systems. In the long run such methods are doomed to failure. Power, riches and success are merely anodynes used by the personality to disguise its own vulnerable condition. The cult of personality itself results in the selection of drugs which increase and render more deadly its state of self-intoxication. What happens to the patient when in age the purchase of a new hat cannot enhance a beauty which has long faded, or when dwindling powers can no longer provide the comforting mirage of further successes?

In our own country the particular fallacies of the personality-cult and the mania for self-expression are rendered more deadly by the social pattern imposed by the Welfare State. Though the latter has alleviated much distress and suffering, in the long run the harm it will do will far outweigh the good. There are signs already that it is wreaking havoc in the spiritual sphere. The whole implication of the system is that life is better than it can be. So many of the services devoted to vocational guidance and the adjustment of circumstances to suit the individual are based on the assumption that if man can only receive the correct professional and social environment for his development, his happiness can be automatically assured. This pathetic fallacy is a hang-over from nineteenth century liberalism. No political party can afford to lose votes by resisting a view which has already been proved wrong to any observer not influenced by political bias or necessity. It is debatable whether standards of honour and morality have declined in the last two decades. In the opinion of the author there is no doubt that they have. What cannot be argued is that people are more tense, less happy and more neurotic than they were. If the safest prescription for peace is submission to one's lot, the scrambling for benefits which goes on in a Welfare State cannot make for anything other than individual unhappiness as well as general anarchy. Transient pleasure may be derived from contemplation of the latest grab but increased hope of material prosperity among those whose lives are devoid of spiritual foundation leads only in the long run to neurosis and despair.

One of the more addled exploits of political theory is the discovery that democracy and fair shares for all is applied Christianity. This is an insidious but deadly blasphemy. Every religion worth the name has predicted that the Kingdom of God is within us. If this fundamental basis of all religions is accepted the effect is to minimize rather than to accentuate the spiritual importance of the environment. The acid test of emotional balance as well as of religious experience is the equanimity with which one accepts one's lot. That welfare schemes should be employed for the alleviation of human suffering is right and proper. Even then, when we are weighing their merits, we should consider, too, the corruption and wastage which goes with them and the opportunities they afford to power-intoxicated officials to do incidental good with deliberately bad intentions. But when the political cult of welfare is regarded as intrinsically good and a way of life in itself one has to point out that far from being the practical application of Christianity it is its direct antithesis. 'Take no thought for your life, what ye shall eat, nor for your body, what ye shall put on.' Thousands of officials are, in the name of ethics, blinding us to the fact that the teachings of Christ are not only more spiritual but more psychiatrically sound than the materialistic enlightenment of the exponents of welfare.

When we consider the emphasis on self-expression and the obsessional desire to avoid frustration which is its consequence one wonders whether, after all, the application of Freudian principles has not done more harm than good. There is no doubt that, applied within the sphere of medicine, they have brought comfort and increased happiness to those individuals with sufficient culture and insight to benefit by them. This is surely an enormous boon, even though the numbers of those benefited is small in relation to the total number of the neurotically sick. But when one considers the effect of Freudian doctrine when disseminated through the whole community, and naturally somewhat perverted in the process, one is more doubtful. There can be no doubt that Freudian theory has been one of the major factors in removing the shackles from humanity. In the history of psychology, or even modern philosophy, it is something more than equivalent to the storming of the Bastille. This analogy, indeed, is particularly apt, because we have exchanged the conventional stability of our former inhibited existence for the chaotic insecurity of free expression. We have, indeed, stepped out of the frying pan into the fire. Both our former codified righteousness and our present state of ethical anarchy are based on the sanctions imposed on us by the herd. In the pre-Freudian era we bowed to the dictates of herd conscience. In our present condition we revolt against them. We have been conducting a civil war on the plane of personality but because our operations have never penetrated to the deeper strata of being we are even worse off than before. That part of our nature which is capable of communion with the Absolute is its own conscience. Conscience, as we commonly understand it, is a mere cowardly compromise between our social and instinctive beings. Freud is incapable of leading us from the morass in which we are floundering because, to him, religious experience is illusory and conscience the mere state of compromise which makes cowards of us all.

III

THE ACTION OF DRUGS

Another dubious tendency in present-day treatment concerns the action of drugs. In the Health Service a great deal of money is being spent on the prescription of new tranquillizers, many of doubtful benefit, and on well-established sedatives of more positive value. Because of the enormous administrative wastage in the Health Service it is only natural that the authorities should aim at economy. Bureaucracy being what it is, it is almost inevitable that the target should be ill-chosen and should be directed at what is, after all, some kind of attempt to treat the patient.

There is a current fashion among younger psychiatrists to write papers on the non-usefulness of the new tranquillizers. Many of the researches unnecessarily celebrated in these papers run to a pattern. A limited number of patients is given a new tranquillizer. An equal number of controls receive a harmless placebo. With so many young psychiatrists seeking preferment and inoculated with the Weltanschauung of the Ministry, the result is a foregone conclusion. The placebo is found to be almost as useful or even more useful than the tranquillizer. These findings are by no means remarkable and it is a pity that their regular repetition occupies so much space in the medical journals. Any form of treatment in which the psychiatrist believes will, given time, produce improvement in a reasonable proportion of his patients. Conversely, any treatment in which he does not believe is likely to prove useless. In addition, many of the new tranquillizers have failed to live up to the claims made for them. Their disappearance from the prescription lists may be no great tragedy. But what one fears is that this sceptism as to the value of drugs may extend to such sheet anchors of treatment as the barbiturates. There are still doctors of puritanical inclination who are disinclined to prescribe them. No one who has read regularly the pages of the *British Medical Journal* can fail to observe the periodic eruption of letters from troubled practitioners for whom the prescription of sedatives (and also analgesics) is anathema. Little protest is raised against the prescription of tonics. These are, like cold baths, hockey, lettuce and evangelicalism, intrinsically healthy. There is little outcry against the ridiculous over-prescription of antibiotics for trivial maladies, though the potential dangers of these are now being realized. But when we come to the question of sedatives and to a less extent of pain-killers the matter is entirely different. The trouble is that the sedative during its period of action can alter appreciably the mood and outlook of the individual. For reasons not easy to explain this is regarded as sinister. The aim of the sedative is to diminish fear and of the analgesic to abolish pain. Fear and pain are the two major influences assisting in the demarcation of personality. The individual in the grip of panic or physical agony is aware as never before of the unique apartness of his personality. The aim of these two varieties of drug is to reduce the patient's acute awareness of himself to more normal proportions.

Now this is the function of all drugs and indeed of all forms of therapy. The antibiotic which combats infection will ultimately reduce the fever, tachycardia, sweating and pain associated with it. In so doing it will return the patient to his normal state of self-awareness. The sedatives and analgesics are suspect because their effect on the personality of the individual is more immediate. Anything which reduces our awareness of personality beyond a certain point is regarded with suspicion in Western civilization. On the contrary soporifics, anodynes and mood-affecting drugs have been used more freely in Eastern systems of medicine than our own.[4] In addition, the Easterner has been able to absorb more of these drugs without ill effect than his Western counterpart.

The aim of the sedative is to enable the patient to take the first step towards reducing his heightened self-awareness to

[4] It should not be forgotten, however, that some of the Eastern religions and philosophical schools are opposed to the use of drugs.

normal. All medicines are artificial re-educators of the psyche. They are necessary to individuals who because of their tension are unable to initiate this process themselves. Prayer and fasting were necessary to mediaeval man when he wished to pass from normal self-awareness to self-annihilation. Sedatives are necessary for modern man when he wishes to reduce his hypertrophied self-awareness to normal proportions. Because so much illness is psychogenic in causation is no argument for reducing the all too inadequate armoury employed for its relief. The present organization of medicine does not permit the widespread teaching of techniques of relaxation nor does it provide an adequate number of psychiatrists to deal with the mass of patients requiring treatment. At the present juncture the widespread use of sedatives is absolutely essential. It is quite possible, however, that the new system of treatment by government edict may suggest a reduction in their application.

The practitioner very commonly fears that the patient may become addicted to the sedatives prescribed for him. Addiction to barbiturates is rare and where it occurs it cannot be described as more catastrophic than addiction to acute agitation. But in any case drug addiction has its origins in the patient and not the drug. The addict is seeking always to escape from the acute self-awareness which is a torture to him. This is well seen in the case of alcoholics who are notoriously self-conscious in their relations with their fellows and who use alcohol as a lubricant facilitating social intercourse. Alcoholics of what used to be called the favoured classes very commonly find relief in drinking with those of an inferior social position. The combination of alcohol and the company of their social inferiors enables them to lose a little their conception of themselves as isolated and vulnerable entities. I have said before that every drug addict has been regarded as a potential mystic. If this is so the addict is essentially a mystic with a difference. Most potential mystics have some inborn capacity for self-annihilation. The drug addict has, as well as the urge to self-annihilation, the initial handicap of a heightened self-consciousness.

It should be remembered that anything which tides over the period of his acute symptoms is probably the most important factor in the treatment of the patient. This is true whether the agent applied is drugs, psychotherapy, electric convulsive treatment, or simply listening to his symptoms without sitting in judgement upon him. When we say that time is the great healer we mean that in the course of its flow the patient learns to submit to his symptoms rather than to revolt against them. No man ever recovered from an illness by 'fighting against it' because, in so doing, he would be fighting against himself and a house divided against itself cannot stand. Anything which reduces the patient's general tension while he is learning the art of submission to his symptoms is of great therapeutic value.

We are seeing the beginnings of a tendency to dispense with drugs. This may be a step in the right direction but the step is precipitate. The view, found more often in general physicians than psychiatrists, that an explanation of the origin of the patient's condition is more important than its symptomatic relief, is a pathetic fallacy. No illness was ever cured by an explanation. It is fantastic to believe that what is an expression of the whole man can be cured by an intellectual exercise on the part of his physician. There is always a considerable interval between the patient's intellectual appreciation of his problems and his emotional adjustment to them.

IV

PRIESTS AND DOCTORS

The question arises as to what degree priests and doctors will be able to co-operate in the future for the relief of disease. In this book we are considering only the question of psychiatric illness but what is written in this chapter could apply equally well to physical maladies. The possibility of co-operation depends on the discovery of fundamental factors on which both parties can agree. I cannot see that there can be any common basis other than a belief in the necessity for self-annihilation. Increased awareness of the personality is a factor common to both psychiatric illness and the varying forms of human misery with which the priest is concerned. The two categories inevitably merge. The melancholic who believes himself to have lost his faith, to be unworthy and to be eternally damned is only exhibiting an extreme manifestation of what is suffered by many in the religious crises associated with their formative years. The sense of apartness is the most important factor common to both psychiatric illness and the spiritual *malaise* with which priests are so often confronted. Is it possible for the priests and doctors to co-operate in measures aimed at the reduction of man's over-acute perception of his own personality?

I do not think we are anywhere near the realization of such an aim and I doubt if it can ever be realized. For a start, it is fantastic to contemplate that the medical profession in the West is anywhere near accepting the principle that it is only by abandonment of belief in the importance of the personality that man can be spared the diseases specifically associated with this concept. Certainly strides have been made in recent years in our understanding of how much disease of all categories can be attributed to emotional conflict, but the methods employed to reduce such conflicts do not as yet express the belief that man must seek to merge with the universal principle before he can shed his load of pathological symptoms.

The obstacles to common action are not provided solely by the medical profession. To what extent does the priesthood itself accept that the principles of submission and self-annihilation are at the basis of religious experience? A minority of mystics may adopt such an attitude but as many or more mystics are found outside the Church as in it and we have no evidence that the priests themselves contribute liberally to their number. I have treated enough priests to know that they are appreciably contaminated with human egoism. A majority in the religious vocation may accept intellectually the principle of self-annihilation but their emotional adjustment to this concept is retarded or lacking. A St Francis de Sales may give advice which by the most rigorous standards measures up to what is required of the most enlightened psychiatrist, but all priests are not St Francis de Sales and all psychiatrists are not enlightened. In addition, while a majority of priests will admit that submission is the basis of religious experience, their admission that this is so is often perfunctory and obviously, to them, of secondary importance to the theological concepts which are the basis of their particular creed.

Hindu systems of thought offer ready-made common ground for the priest and doctor because they are more concerned with the control of mind, emotion and bodily function in the pursuit of spiritual aims. The materialism of Western Medicine and the dogmatic and often exclusive intellectualism of orthodox Christianity are each in their separate ways huge obstacles to the realization, in Western civilization, of such an attitude. The gulf is not that between a materialistic and a spiritual concept of life. It is a clash between two relatively closed systems of thought, both predominantly ratiocinative and scientific. Medicine is declining from an art to the level of a natural science and Christianity, with many honourable exceptions, is confined and mutilated by theological science.

Disease is a protest of the whole man. As such the responsibility for its relief should rest in the hands of a single individual. The value of the doctor to the patient depends on the *rapport* established between them. This is equally true of the relation between the priest and the sinner. The laity often use, or were accustomed to use, the term father confessor to describe the functions of the doctor to whom they confided their troubles. The successful doctor was, indeed, a father figure. One of the most certain guarantees of the future decline of medicine is the fact that you cannot make a father-figure from a subordinate official of the civil service. Perhaps the best the patient can do is to regard him as a diluted version of Big Brother. In those branches of Christianity where confession is an established practice the priest receives the title of Father. For both the doctor and the priest success in his mission depends on the degree of transference he stimulates in the sufferer and in his skill and scrupulousness in managing it. Now sick or sorry, patient or sinner, you cannot with profit exhibit the phenomenon of transference to two Father-figures. This is merely to reproduce in other spheres the contemporary misery of the divided home. The priests and the doctors may co-operate and form a quorum to discuss the principles of treatment on which they are agreed, but transference, if it is to have any curative value, cannot be exhibited towards a committee. In the East the aspirant towards spiritual development is also the apprentice who seeks to control the functions of his body. He is serving an aim which is medical, psychological and spiritual. He places himself not in the hands of doctor, psychiatrist and priest but limits himself to a single being he calls his *guru*. The latter observes his aptitude for the physical and mental techniques prescribed and notes and directs his resulting spiritual development. In the West there is no such whole management of the whole man, and no near prospect of such a culmination. How many doctors are interested even in changes of mood induced by variations in the patient's physical state, let alone in his possibilities of spiritual development by physical and mental techniques? And how many Western ecclesiastics would be content to direct the development of spiritual experience and spiritual powers without exerting intellectual pressure in favour of their own particular theological system?

I have raised this question of the *guru* for the sole purpose of illustrating that there is no analogy between the Eastern one man, total treatment of the whole man and any system of medical and clerical co-operation we are likely to evolve in the West. This is not to say that the Hindu or any other Eastern faith is superior to Christianity, certainly as conceived of by Christ. But it must be accepted that techniques for the total direction of the individual's physical, mental and spiritual development have no counterpart here, nor is there any likelihood that we will evolve any analogous methods within any reasonable period of time. Our doctors are not priests and our priests not doctors. Our nearest approach to such an ideal is the doctor with a simple and not too differentiated sense of religion. One cannot consider the priest in this connection because of his lack of psychiatric or medical knowledge. I am prepared to believe that, suitably interpreted, the Gospels are of all the most useful primers for the study of human psychology. But the interpretation of the Christian message is a controversial issue and only a minority of priests could be expected to accept one expressed in terms of the deeper, psychiatric implications of the Gospels.

In recent years the Roman Church has arranged for the training of a number of priests in the principles of psychoanalysis. This may be a step in the right direction but we cannot be sure. This Church, contrary to superficial belief, has often been most progressive in utilizing for its own purposes new impulses and new knowledge which it considers safe and useful. Perhaps there is no great danger of the principles of psychoanalysis being insidiously amended by clerical practitioners. Even if this occurred it might be no great source for regret because no doctrine is sacred and that of Freud is fallible in several respects. But because of Roman exclusiveness in matters of doctrine one cannot imagine that such therapy would be afforded to anything other than Romans and, if it was, it is hard to believe that the patient would not be indoctrinated, though possible not directly, in the tenets of Roman Catholicism. In any case the fact that the father-figure was a Roman would incline the patient, in the course of his transference, to lean towards that religion. Naturally one is not implying that it is a disaster for anyone to be converted to Romanism but it is futile and potentially dangerous for a patient to have as a father-figure one pledged to any religious system so sharply defined in theological terms as the Roman Church. If a religion is to be of value and to be stabilized in the soul of the individual it must appeal to, and be an expression of, the whole man. The religion of choice must therefore vary with the temperament and cultural development of the individual and in making his choice he must not be exposed to undue influence.

Should civilization surprise us by continuing and itself by even improving, we may one day achieve the conception of the doctor as priest, or better still, the priest as doctor. We should remember that in highly developed civilizations prior to our own men have performed this double function. Against the background of our current beliefs such an idea is ludicrous. Before the days of the National Health Service we practised our calling under a system of free enterprise and in competition with others for financial gain. I am sure that on the whole the profession behaved with considerable honesty. Such money grubbing as occurred was of less moment than the place-hunting and Empire building which has characterized the ornate edifice of the Health Service. But if we are ever to have the priest-doctor both the financial motives and the cult of personal power will be not only undesirable but impracticable. It will take us so long to qualify that only those without financial aspirations or the will to power will ever contemplate entering such a vocation. It is hard to see how the conception of the priest doctor could be established except against the background of something analogous to a monastic system. The acolyte would, after all, have to be clothed, fed and sheltered during the long years of his initiate.

But since we cannot in our civilization produce the doctor-priest, we will, sooner or later, aspire, or be reduced, to the treatment of the patient by both priests and doctors. I cannot regard such a prospect with enthusiasm or even hope. The relief of misery is so dependent on the to and fro impact of the mind and soul of the sufferer on that of the person undertaking its relief. The treatment of the patient by two separate individuals with different outlooks and different intuitive qualities is an unnatural dichotomy which is not likely to produce good results and which in many cases may do harm. But since we live in an age of committees we may as well form a sub-committee on salvation. At any rate there is every indication that such a state of affairs will soon be realized. After all, a great deal of Western religious and philosophic thought is of such a nature as to aid in the realization of this combined medical and clerical approach. During most of its existence, Christianity has regarded the body as an undesirable black sheep dragged along, from a sense of duty, by its more respectable siblings, the mind and soul. The scope of an approach which regards man as composed of three more or less clearly definable essences is naturally more limited than it otherwise could be. The trouble is that, though the materialism of medicine is leading towards an *impasse*, doctors are, as a whole, more capable than priests of the necessarily total approach to the suffering. This is for the simple reason that, except possibly in some of the Roman orders, the training of priests in the study of the mind is not comprehensive and their knowledge of the body is no better than that of the average layman.

It should also be remembered that the Cartesian dualism envisages an extreme degree of separation between the two entities of mind and body. This philosophic system must be completely untenable to anyone with the slightest knowledge of modern medicine. Yet the crude principle of the domination of mind over matter[5] still influences the thought of many Europeans. It may have been abandoned by the philosophers

[5] This is an entirely different proposition from the training of the mind and its utilization in the control of bodily functions, which is practised in some of the Eastern systems.

themselves but it remains, like a piece of isolated sea wrack, as the one philosophical acquisition of those not philosophically minded. Such secular thinking would also, in our Western civilization, pre-dispose to the piecemeal treatment of the patient by a medico-clerical barrage. We may therefore confront the future, unlike the French officer before Waterloo, with fear and perhaps a little hope.

The dangers involved in co-operation between doctors, or more especially psychiatrists, and priests is considerable. The greatest is that the latter may either deliberately or inadvertently increase that sense of guilt which is still widely held to be part of the basis of Christianity. According to my own interpretation of Christ's teaching its aims would be similar to that of psychiatry in this particular matter of guilt feelings. But the idea that Christ came to take away the sins of the world and that remorse, but not repentance, can and often is morbid and irreligious, is not generally accepted by the Church. It is, indeed, strongly refuted by the more Calvinist sects. It would be tempting to say that the danger of the priest increasing the patient's sense of guilt is greater among those of Evangelical than among those of Catholic persuasion. I think this is on the whole true but one cannot believe for a moment that such tactics are solely the prerogative of the Protestant Left. At any rate, from whatever quarter it comes, to increase the sense of guilt of a self-accusing and hyperconscientious depressive is a grave responsibility.

Another considerable danger is that people other than psychiatrists are often too ambitious and hurried in their dealings with neurotic patients. There is a tendency to believe that once the patient's difficulties and failings have been explained to him he should immediately begin to recover. Too many people try to hole out in one at the patient's expence. The aim of psychiatric treatment is to enable the patient to mature emotionally and this is inevitably a slow process. Mere intellectual insight into his problem is not enough. Ideally the patient should be enabled to educate himself. This often means that he must go at his own pace. To confront him too early with unpalatable facts about himself is often to wound him unnecessarily and to arouse his antagonism. A psychiatrist should be a good listener. A voluble psychiatrist is as much a clanging cymbal as a talking judge. It is only human nature that the amateur, in dealing with the psychiatrically sick, should be more Roman than the Romans and talk more than is advisable.

On the whole it is better if the psychiatrist, having failed with the potentially religious patient, hands him over completely to the consolation of religion. In so doing he should satisfy himself that the priest concerned is a man of humanity and insight. If he can find a priest whose main concern is the healing effect of religious experience then so much the better. He should at least ensure that his patient avoids those false prophets who believe that there is a single theological prescription for the cure of all human ills. A great deal too much is made of the example of those who are said to have solved their difficulties by submitting to the discipline of the more authoritarian religious systems. In our civilization the claim of a cure-all is more likely to be made on behalf of the Roman Catholic Church than any other. No doubt there are many who have found within its fellowship a peace which they failed to achieve in the communities in which they were nurtured or in the agnosticism or atheism into which they had foundered. I doubt whether the peace they have achieved is to be attributed to any submission to the theological principles of that religion. It is more likely that, for them, the atmosphere of Romanism was conducive to the more total process of self-surrender. If the patient must leave the psychiatrist, let him seek aid from those who believe, without too much regard for theological minutae, that healing is divine in origin, that the priest is merely its earthly channel and that it is in no sense a sectarian attribute.

Earlier in this section I suggested that what mankind needs is the priest-doctor. I make this suggestion, unrealisable though it is in our civilization, because I see no other means of furthering the concept of the doctor as healer. By this latter term I imply that the doctor would himself be endowed with intrinsic powers of healing. It is only against the background of religion that such a view could be accepted as orthodox. In the early centuries the healing of the sick was one of the obligations laid on the Christian. The Church today has shown that it is prepared to tolerate and even encourage such activities. It is indisputable that the systems of faith and spiritual healing which are practised today have a much closer liaison with the Church than with the medical profession. But the conception of the doctor as healer cannot flourish in the atmosphere of materialism which stifles present-day medicine. The modern doctor is essentially a vehicle for the application of certain scientific principles which become increasingly more rigid. Again, we are moving towards the view that one doctor is the same as another. We see this in practice in the big combines where the patient has no guarantee that on his separate visits to the surgery he may not see each of the four or five brethren in turn. The patient who sees one surgeon at out-patients very often entrusts his life in the operating theatre to a stranger whom he has not seen previously. The pattern of treatment is increasingly laid down for us in pamphlets issued by the Ministry of Health for whom, presumably, the disease response of an individual who likes the Fifth Symphony is the same as that of his confrere who believes what his M.P. tells him. Against such a background we are not likely to look with favour on the idea that the doctor may be endowed with intrinsic powers of healing. The tragedy of the situation is that, while the profession as a whole sets its face rigidly against such an idea, the vast majority of our patients endorse it completely. A doctor is naïve indeed who imagines that his patients judge him by the same scientific standards which he sets for himself.

There is nothing magical or even remarkable in the idea that there are doctors whose intrinsic powers of healing are greatly in excess of their fellows. Some soldiers are more greatly endowed with a capacity for leadership than others. The born teacher can incite children to learn whereas his colleagues may fail totally to do so. What is extraordinary is that the profession should have set its face so rigidly against the concept of intrinsic healing powers. This may be due in part to the fact that doctors begin to specialize in natural science subjects as early as fifteen and that as time goes on the profession is more and more recruited from those whose general education is poor and whose cultural background is inadequate. The inclasticity of the concepts of natural science are a pitiable equipment for those destined to guide their fellows in pain and sorrow. But this is not the sole explanation and it is possible that, at deeper levels of consciousness than those concerned with the desire for money and power, we have a vested interest in the continuance of disease. It can be argued that in pneumonia penicillin will be equally efficacious whatever doctor injects it, but it is dangerous to quote the case of infectious conditions in such an argument. This variety of illness is essentially a less complicated response than the stress diseases. It would be unduly bold to assert that the response of these latter is independent of the nature of the doctor in charge. I am not referring to the skill and tact with which the latter applies himself to the treatment of his patient but to his own essential essence. The outlook in many functional illnesses depends enormously on the nature, as distinct from the capacities, of the first doctor who handles them. Nor should it be forgotten that the most successful physicians are often the most silent. Their effect on their patients depends less on their words than on themselves. It is a cardinal error to believe that the new school who lecture the patient frankly as to the nature of his symptoms are necessarily successful. Of course a great deal depends on whether the doctor exerts positive or negative suggestion. He may be a positive and reassuring remover of symptoms or a negative and lugubrious inducer of them. But quite apart from the enormous element of suggestion, it is possible that the doctor can, knowingly or unknowingly, and almost always the latter, bring healing to the patient, or retard its course.

After all, it is difficult to avoid the conclusion that, outside the profession, individuals have healing powers. If we take the simple example of massage, the results obtained by some workers are far in excess of those obtained by others and to a degree which cannot be explained by variations in the degree of anatomical knowledge or technical skill on the part of the masseur in question. Few doctors would dispute the truth of this assertion. The better results obtained by some can, of course, be explained by the fact that these individuals have a better touch than their less gifted fellows. But the gift of a good touch is an intrinsic quality. It may be developed by practice but it is essentially an innate endowment of the individual and a localized expression of his whole personality. Again, in instructing a patient in the art of relaxation, the results obtained by different individuals are enormously variable. It is difficult to conceive of some individuals, in virtue of their own innate tension, ever succeeding in obtaining the desired results. In this particular branch of treatment the voice of the therapist is of immense importance, being, after all, the main weapon in his therapeutic armoury. Of all things the voice is among the most individual assets possessed by any human being. Nor can it be disputed that the voice is an expression, and often the most revealing, of the individual's personality. We cannot deny the influence of these unique and personal attributes in the case of the masseur and the instructor in the art of relaxation. How then can we minimize the importance of intrinsic healing attributes in those who practice the possibly more complex art of medicine?

A medical colleague of mine tells me of the existence through several generations of a family of the art of wart charming. This trivial and seemingly ludicrous example is of great importance in relation to our present theme. If skill in this particular subspeciality—perhaps it will be taken up by the National Health Service and may earn somebody a merit award—consisted in the muttering of incantations we could attribute the cures obtained to the effects of suggestion on individuals particularly susceptible to it. But no magic formulae are repeated and no herbal concoctions applied. The patient is merely told that the wart will get better and it does. This happens where the remedies of the doctors have failed repeatedly. The wart disappears without leaving a scar. Can we explain this by the tendency of some warts to recede of their own account? No, because their disappearance occurs in a week or two after the visit to the wart charmer and subsequent to their obstinate persistence for much longer periods. The obdurately scientific doctor may still persist that the cure is obtained by suggestion and that, even if no incantations are uttered, a silent variety of this mechanism is utilized for the patient's benefit. This involves the belief that the grandfather, father and son of a working-class family are all endowed with a particular gift of cure by suggestion. This is more than most people will be prepared to swallow. One cannot conceive that such an explanation would satisfy any but the more gullible among those doctors whose loyalty to scientific principles is combined with a capacity for remoteness which is ill-suited to their cultivation of what is called hard sense.

Do we accept the fact that Christ was able to heal the sick and that for two or three centuries after His coming this office was one of the basic requirements of the Christian? The answer to this question must depend on the degree to which the individual leans towards a belief in the reality of religious experience or towards the principles of nineteenth century rationalism. Attempts have been made to bridge the gap between these two schools of thought by asserting that Christ was a kind of early psychiatrist who had remarkable success with hysterics. It is implied that the people He cured were in the main cases of hysteria masquerading as organic illness. This is the sort of argument based on faith and convenience which is more usually the error of the religiously inclined. It is a curious fact that among the many categories of neurosis, hysteria is the most resistant to treatment. We have all heard of cases of hysteria cured in five minutes but I suspect that a large number of these were not hysterics but more or less conscious malingerers. Brilliant results with hysterics may have been obtained at the first attempt by old-fashioned brusque neurologists, but I doubt whether the patients returned very often to the same authorities when they relapsed next day.

The evidence that certain individuals in different ages and civilizations have been endowed with healing power is very compelling. If we accept this as factual we may seem unduly credulous. On the other hand, if we dismiss it out of hand, we are committing the no less grave error of being blindly incredulous. If we reject what has been described as happening in a previous century we are doing so on the grounds that it could not be possible. In short, we are dismissing what might have been a fact because we think it could not have been a fact. This is, in terms of ordinary sense, an utterly illogical attitude. Its confused nature is often disguised by the cloak of a pseudo-scientific attitude which makes its own rules and dismisses as impossible anything the existence of which it finds difficult to explain.

We are on much firmer ground if we can investigate in our own time the claims of the faith and spiritual healers. I understand that the cures at Lourdes are examined carefully by a committee of orthodox medical practitioners and that the criteria enabling a case to be regarded as cured are strict. I do not know. The most authentic case of which I have heard was of a woman with a carcinoma, verified by X-rays, who was seen by a colleague of mine and written off as incurable. To his own amazement he saw her some years afterwards, perfectly recovered and having attended a faith healer in the interval. My colleague was the senior and most distinguished physician at the main hospital in his locality. He had an international reputation in his speciality. He was cautious in the practice of his craft, highly endowed with common sense and so far as I could tell not in the least religious. He was in no doubt that the patient he had seen was cured.

I do not know whether the profession is prepared to accept such facts as these. One would have thought that if it is prepared to believe that a whirlwind of disc lesions and cases of hiatus hernia appeared immediately after these two conditions had been defined it would be prepared to accept anything. But at least we should not fall back on the ready-made explanation of spontaneous remissions. This is good enough for asthma, schizophrenia and possibly thread worms. It is somewhat inadequate when applied to a mortal illness.

I have mentioned briefly the evidence for what one may perhaps crudely term non-medical healing simply to demonstrate that healing powers may exist in individuals unarmed by the pharmacological and even psychological artifices of medicine. The religious may insist that such powers are not innate or intrinsic in the individual but are manifestations of the Holy Spirit in him. But the point at issue is not the origin of the healing power but that it exists independent of any medical knowledge or skill and possibly even of any special intuitive capacity. Now what I have written in the last few paragraphs may not seem especially enlightened and may even appear obvious, but what is of interest and perhaps of remarkable significance is that we as a profession are more resistant to such facts than most sections of the community. Our resistance is all the more remarkable when we consider that ours was known as the healing art. Or perhaps, after all, it is not so remarkable. We are now prouder of the term the science of medicine. Healing has become slightly old-fashioned and living at peace with one's symptoms is all the rage. If, contrary to the omens, civilization persists and even develops, we will find that an art of healing beyond the present scope of medicine will be developed. It may even be that the training of the apprentice may include the development of such healing powers.

INDEX

GEORGE ALLEN & UNWIN LTD
London: 40 Museum Street, W.C.1

Auckland: 24 Wyndham Street
Bombay: 15 Graham Road, Ballard Estate, Bombay 1
Calcutta: 17 Chittaranjan Avenue, Calcutta 13
Cape Town: 109 Long Street
Karachi: Metherson's Estate, Wood Street, Karachi 2
New Delhi: 13-14 Ajmeri Gate Extension, New Delhi 1
Sao Paulo: Avenida 9 de Julho 1138-Ap. 51
Singapore, South East Asia & Far East, 36c, Princep Street
Sydney, N.S.W.: Bradbury House, 55 York Street
Toronto: 91 Wellington Street West

www.ingramcontent.com/pod-product-compliance
Ingram Content Group UK Ltd.
Pitfield, Milton Keynes, MK11 3LW, UK
UKHW020204200926
475702UK00004B/600
* 9 7 8 0 4 1 5 7 1 7 1 0 6 *